AWAY WITH WORDS

Young Writers' 16th Annual Poetry Competition

It is feeling and force of imagination that make us eloquent.

How can I not dream while writing? The blank page gives a right to dream.

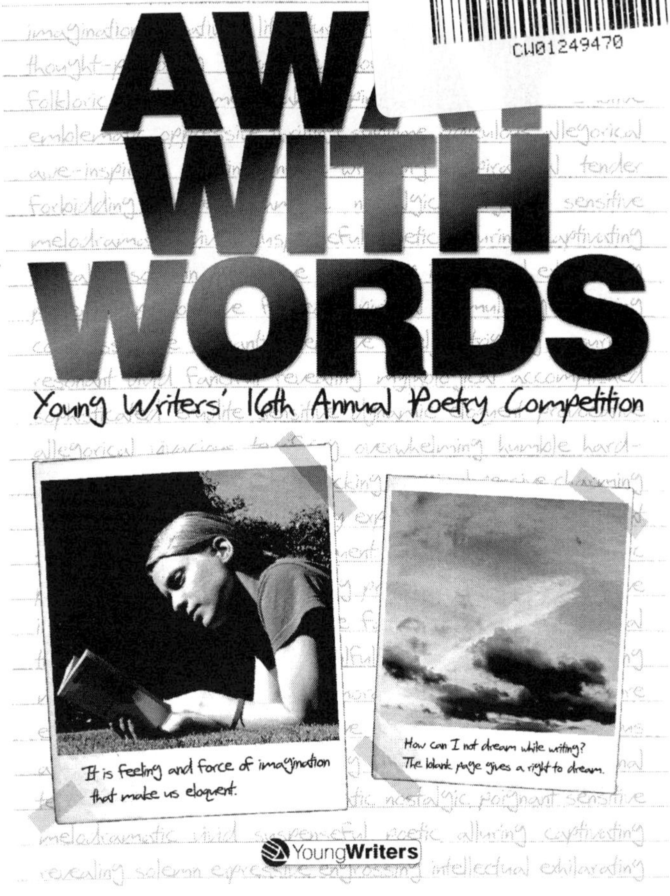

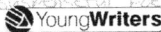

Inspirations From Wales
Edited by Allison Jones

First published in Great Britain in 2007 by:
Young Writers
Remus House
Coltsfoot Drive
Peterborough
PE2 9JX
Telephone: 01733 890066
Website: www.youngwriters.co.uk

All Rights Reserved

© Copyright Contributors 2007

SB ISBN 978-1 84602 868 7

Foreword

This year, the Young Writers' *Away With Words* competition proudly presents a showcase of the best poetic talent selected from thousands of up-and-coming writers nationwide.

Young Writers was established in 1991 to promote the reading and writing of poetry within schools and to the young of today. Our books nurture and inspire confidence in the ability of young writers and provide a snapshot of poems written in schools and at home by budding poets of the future.

The thought, effort, imagination and hard work put into each poem impressed us all and the task of selecting poems was a difficult but nevertheless enjoyable experience.

We hope you are as pleased as we are with the final selection and that you and your family continue to be entertained with *Away With Words Inspirations From Wales* for many years to come.

Contents

Bryn Hafren Comprehensive School, Barry
Jennifer Rushton (12)	1
Jessica Jenkins (12)	2
Sophie Jones (12)	3
Cheyenne Whitlock	4
Emma Meyrick (14)	5
Joely Walker (12)	6
Jannat Ahmed (11)	7
Laura Davies (13)	8
Jadine Procope (12)	9
Jazmin Howell (12)	10
Stacey Davies (12)	11
Alex Curran (14)	12
Emily Claydon (12)	13
Leasha Davies (11)	14
Charlotte Ferris (11)	15
Siobhain Cahill (11)	16
Lauren Gomes (11)	17
Lauren Avianne Tallemach (13)	18

Hartridge High School, Newport
Charmaine Selwood (13)	19
Stacey Jones (11)	20
Ryan O'Connor (12)	21
Jamil Choudory (11)	22
Thomas Hill (11)	23
Yvonne Fleet (11)	24
Daniel Kiely (11)	25
Mahammed Adel Saad (13)	26
Ryan Johnson (13)	27
Jason Little (13)	28
Josh Poole (13)	29
Daneka Cheshire (12)	30
Thomas Llewellyn (12)	31
Francesca Morris (11)	32
Kieron Campbell (12)	33
Steven Taylor (13)	34
Jamie Warner (11)	35
Jacob Huish	36

Kayleigh Poole (11)	37
Bethan Spruce (12)	38
Chanice Edwards (11)	39
Jamie Derrick (12)	40
Taher Mansfield (11)	41
Paige Jones (12)	42
Nikita Evans (11)	43
Kirsty Knorz (12)	44
Bethan Clayton (11)	45
Tammarah Fowler (11)	46
Ellesse Buss (13)	47
Alex O'Neill (13)	48
Benjamin Shatford (13)	49
Matthew Kerslake (13)	50
Harriet Smith (13)	51
Charlie Ford (12)	52
Rebecca Bill (13)	53
Hannah Shingler (12)	54
Megan Bliss (12)	55
Andrew Wright (12)	56
Hollie Short (13)	57
Benjamin Jones (12)	58
Mandy Harvey (12)	59
Emily Campbell (12)	60
Rhiannon Elizabeth Tucker (12)	61
Elicia Collins (12)	62
Josh Allsopp (12)	63
Daniel Dervin (12)	64
Shadine Evans (12)	65
Natalie Bevan (13)	66
James Pitt (12)	67
Hannah Bishop (12)	68
Kayleigh Lewis (13)	69
Seana O'Driscoll (12)	70
Hannah Giles (12)	71
Ashleigh Lloyd	72
Callum Tufft (11)	73
Aimee Rees (12)	74
Joshua Stock	75
Leighton Phillips)	76
Joshua Sweet (11)	77
Shannon Trigg (11)	78

Louise Tamplin (11)	79
Bonnie Arlett (12)	80
Natalie West (13)	81
Jessica Evans (12)	82
Leigh Derrick (12)	83
Mark O'Connell (12)	84
Amy Mansfield (13)	85
Kirsty Louise Willis (11)	86
Shawn James (12)	87
Liam Codd (12)	88
Matthew Tucker (12)	89
Vicki-Marie Richardson (12)	90
Oliver Griffiths (12)	91
Paige Attewell (13)	92
Zak Yearsley (13)	93
Chelsea Toms (12)	94
Carysann Fowler (12)	95
Ryan Everett (12)	96
Ashley Edmunds (12)	97

Ruthin School, Ruthin

Luke Retout (13)	98
Adam Roberts (13)	99
Charlotte Baugh (12)	100
Ashley Griffiths (13)	101
Ellie Birkett (11)	102
Dafydd Atkinson (13)	103
Catherine Jones	104
Lorna Elizabeth Drake (13)	105
Lara Pritchard (13)	106
Alexander Dowell (11)	107
Robin Pritchard (11)	108
George De Vera Davey (11)	109
Ashley Burrows Brown (12)	110
Holly Morris (12)	111
Ruairidh Kerrigan (12)	112

St Gerard's School Trust, Bangor

Robert Jones (12)	113
Amber Langford (12)	114
Freya Nedderman (12)	115

Apryl Fell (12)	116
Matthew Motley (12)	117
Ben Jones (12)	118
Anna Mathiesen (12)	119
Morfydd Thomas (13)	120
Katrina Jenkinson (13)	121
Rosie Lowe (13)	122
Rose Sutton (14)	123
Tanya Duffy (13)	124
Jessica Watters (13)	125
Charlotte Taylorson-Smith-Pritchard (13)	126
Jaimie Whiteley (13)	127
Radha Patel (13)	128
Harriet Silcocks (13)	129
Laura Havens (13)	130
Alex Brown (13)	131
Caleb Allport (12)	132
Blanca Bennett (12)	133
Nicole Pearson (11)	134
India Hill (12)	135
Hannale Niesser (11)	136
Phoebe Lofts (11)	137
Jodie Marley (11)	138
Olivia Roberts (11)	139
Anna Jones (11)	140
Jessica Stanmore (11)	141
Eve Aron (12)	142
Tom Niesser (12)	143
Olivia Farmanbar (12)	144
Sarah Owen (12)	145
Lucy Spain (12)	146
Jessica Hannah Vicars (12)	147
Morgan Gould (12)	148
Edward James Frost (13)	149
Sioned Williams (12)	150
Elin Dawson (12)	151
Sara Jane Jones (13)	152
Morgan Teal (12)	153
Faizan Asad (12)	154
Aya Maria Abdulmawla (12)	155
Jordan Anderson (11)	156
Owain Fraser-Williams (12)	157

Jack Allport (12)	158
Grace Taylorson-Smith-Pritchard (11)	159
Jessica Waddy (11)	160
Bethan Mair Humphreys (11)	161
Sacha Healey (11)	162
Alana Maerivoet (11)	163
Katie Moules-Jones (11)	164
Bryony Jayne Rodger (11)	165
Becky Hill (13)	166
Nia Owen (12)	167
Claire Fell (12)	168

Ysgol Gyfun Gwynllyw, Pontypool

Dylan Davies (11)	169
Grace Williams (11)	170
Abbie Rebecca Jones (11)	171
Emily Dicken (12)	172
Evie Gill (11)	173
Bethan Machado (13)	174
Azaria Davies-House (13)	176
Saran Wyburn (13)	177
Jake Phillips (12)	178
Chris Williamson (12)	180
Jack Bell (12)	181
Carys Rose Puw (12)	182
Joanne Simms (12)	183
Amy Davies (12)	184
Megan Preece (12)	185
Gabriella Sara Jones (13)	186
Kathryn Kelleher (13)	188
Paige Hannah Godwin (12)	189
Rosie Kelleher (13)	190

Ysgol Gyfun Llanhari, Pontyclun

Hollie Simon (17)	191
Eleanor Rose West (16)	192
Ashley John (14)	194

The Poems

Child Abuse

Thoughts circled her brain,
Not wanting to come home
And relive that pain.

She knew what was waiting when she opened the door,
A fist or maybe a chair,
No one knew why she'd come to school feeling sore.

It's the same every day,
'You're rubbish, you're nothing,'
People will say.

Some days broken ribs, other's black eyes,
Someone must stop this,
Don't just sit there and sigh.

Jennifer Rushton (12)
Bryn Hafren Comprehensive School, Barry

Child Abuse

I'm here if you want me,
I'm here all alone,
I hear you shouting at my mum on the phone.

She's not home till later,
You don't want her to see,
The way you always beat me.

I come down to see what's wrong,
You punch me away,
I curl in the corner,
You kick me every day.

I tell you I love you,
You tell me you don't,
I tell you I need you,
You tell me don't.

I ask you to be nice,
You tell me you won't,
I tell you I'm sorry,
You drag me upstairs.

Mummy is back,
I hide when you eat your tea,
I love you Mum and Dad
And I run away.

Jessica Jenkins (12)
Bryn Hafren Comprehensive School, Barry

Animal Abuse

I sit at home,
Waiting for my owner,
He drinks in a pub,
He's a sad, pathetic loner.

He slams the door,
It's late at night,
He's in a mood,
Probably been in a fight.

He's stamping his feet,
I get out the way,
I run to my bed,
Lay there and pray.

He stamps over to me,
I think I'm going to die,
I squeal in pain,
As he slaps me in the eye.

I hate him so much,
He gives me so much pain,
Why does he do it?
What can he gain?

He hits my belly,
It hurts so much,
I feel like I'm dying,
It's too sore to touch.

I wish someone could hear,
I wish I had a voice,
He shouts at me for barking,
But really I don't make a noise.

I wish he would love me,
But that would be a fantasy.

Sophie Jones (12)
Bryn Hafren Comprehensive School, Barry

Child Abuse

I'm here on my own,
No one to hold me,
I'm here on my own,
They all say I'm ugly.

Why can't they love me?
All they do is hate,
I am so lonely,
God I'm only eight.

I have no brothers or sisters,
No company at all,
You burnt me and gave me blisters,
I had to hide away in the hall.

I have a black eye cos of you,
You beat me black and blue,
You even hit me when I was two,
But I still love you.

You gave me no meals,
No food, not a drop of water
And my daddy steals,
But I would hate to think of slaughter.

I see people on the adverts,
Crying and pleading.

Cheyenne Whitlock
Bryn Hafren Comprehensive School, Barry

My Life

I feel unlike other kids,
I creep so carefully around the house,
Afraid that I will wake my dad,
If I do, there will be hell,
He will throw me out of my room.

As I slowly pack my bag, I hear a noise and start to cry,
He is coming down the stairs, did I wake him?
I run to hide but what's the use, he always finds me
One way or the other,
My only hope is to tell someone but if Dad finds out,
There's no use for me to live.

I'm only ten;
I deserve better,
To have a life of my own,
Where my dad helps me with my homework,
Where my parents are together again.

I love my school and my friends,
I feel so safe surrounded by my friends,
I stay late some nights to have some fun,
Cos when I get home the fun ends.

He tells me to get out of his sight,
He takes all my books and pens,
He tells me that I'm stupid and dumb,
But something inside of me says, *'No!'*

Emma Meyrick (14)
Bryn Hafren Comprehensive School, Barry

My Life

I'm 13, my thoughts are cold,
The prison is dark,
They've taken my home,
My brothers, my sisters are far from me,
Like my hopes and my dreams.

An empty pit is pulling me in,
The hunger, the suffering,
The empty feeling,
My voice is gone,
So no hope there,
I'll be here forever, that can't be fair.

The light is fading,
I'm growing cold,
Will I live? No one knows,
The pain is endless,
Let me die,
They continue the torture,
Oh why, oh why?

Joely Walker (12)
Bryn Hafren Comprehensive School, Barry

Harry Potter And Friends

Harry, Hermione and of course Ron,
Put all together, make a trio of fun,
They are wizards and witches,
They fight together on Quidditch pitches,
They go to Hogwarts which is great,
But Harry and Ron are always late.

Jannat Ahmed (11)
Bryn Hafren Comprehensive School, Barry

Away With Words

Nasty words are always said,
They stay with you until you're dead,
You keep the cruelty locked inside,
You want to go away and hide,
Waiting for someone to save your life,
When at your throat, there is a knife.

Solitary confinement, time drags on,
My days of freedom are long gone,
I have no voice, but so much to say,
'Help me please, I cannot stay!'
It feels like I have been in here forever,
My date of release has been scheduled as never.

There is no sound to be heard,
My vision is becoming blurred,
I have never seen light,
Every day, it is a night,
The guard gives me a harsh glare,
Every time I stop and stare.

The only reason I live on,
Is because maybe hope has not gone,
I receive these letters, one, two, three!
It says they've been sent through Amnesty,
So maybe my story has been heard
And people are fighting through the power of words.

Laura Davies (13)
Bryn Hafren Comprehensive School, Barry

Away With Words

I'm here
I'm observing the suffering pain
I'm witnessing the contagious sadness
Dying people hopeless for real life
Injustice, pessimistic
The unpleasantness is burning my eyes
I can't take watching captivity every day
I want to help, I want to give freedom.

I'm here
I'm absorbing the suffering pain
I'm a victim
The sound of children screaming for their parents
Is burning my ears
The smell of putrid sick as pregnant women
And ill kids throw up every minute of the day
Is burning my nose
I wish I could be let free
The special, supporting, caring letters are all I have
In this
Nightmare but they are inspiring and uplifting
And I would do anything
For more and more
Although these metal bars are here
They may be capturing me but they cannot capture my spirit
I may look weak and hopeless but in my heart I will fight
Fight for what is truly mine
Freedom!

Jadine Procope (12)
Bryn Hafren Comprehensive School, Barry

Away With Words

A mnesty International begs for freedom,
W here there's a will there's a way,
A lways beaten and abused,
Y oung people need your help.

W ill anyone come and help us?
I ll people need a doctor,
T he world feels like it's going to end,
H elp lots of people live a normal life.

W here there is help needed, there is no help,
O ur hopes fade every day,
R eal people scared to death,
D rowning their sorrows,
S ave them, save the world.

Jazmin Howell (12)
Bryn Hafren Comprehensive School, Barry

Away With Words

Stop the pain, oh
Please, stop the pain,
But no one can,
You don't really care,
Whereas if it were you,
Then you're care.

Open your eyes, oh
Please, open your eyes,
Maybe you're looking,
But not really seeing,
What they do to us,
You don't see.

Have a heart, oh
Please, have a heart,
I can't take anymore,
None of us can,
The bruises are so bad now,
A fake smile is impossible.

Save us now, oh
Please, save us now,
Our bones are cracked,
From this endless harm,
Soon it'll be so bad,
Our lives will be gone.

Save the children, oh
Please, save the children,
Just spare their lives,
Put yourself in our shoes,
Crying every night,
Partly dying every day, every night.

Help before it's too late, oh
Please, help us now,
Been in here for years,
Is the grass still growing
And the midnight sky?
Say, what's the weather like?

Stacey Davies (12)
Bryn Hafren Comprehensive School, Barry

Away With Words

No tear should make a sound,
No life should be laid on the ground.

When do we stop and stare,
When we can help and care?

Where is the hope and spirit,
That we all crave from above?

When will people realise,
All the world needs is love?

So why do we stop and stare,
When we could help and care?

Alex Curran (14)
Bryn Hafren Comprehensive School, Barry

Amnesty

Wars, wars, wars,
Leaders giving people chores,
Forced to do what you're told,
Locked away until you're old,
Scared and frightened for many years,
Worrying about all your fears,
You're not sure how you'll die,
They will watch you as you cry,
Waiting for your bones to crumble,
You can hear a distant mumble.

Emily Claydon (12)
Bryn Hafren Comprehensive School, Barry

A Fantastic World

A nasty country where no one gets justice,
No laws, no rules, nothing to do.

Just sit there in fear of whether they'll catch you,
Thinking you're the one to blame,
For singing that song yesterday.

Or maybe even writing a letter,
Getting locked up for nothing at all,
Facing a life in prison, you didn't do
Anything at all.

No contact with your family,
Not even farewell, goodbye,
Sentenced to death, for speaking out,
There's nothing you can do.

Leasha Davies (11)
Bryn Hafren Comprehensive School, Barry

Away With Words

A is for amnesty, support them!
W is for the way you to it,
A is for awful, the way they treat you,
Y is for you, you choose.

W is for women suffering violence,
I is for imprisonment,
T is for together, all do join in,
H is for human, they are human too.

W is for worldwide, for all to work as one,
O is for opinions, say your opinion,
R is for rage, your rage,
D is for day, enjoy it,
S is for support, we need your support.

Charlotte Ferris (11)
Bryn Hafren Comprehensive School, Barry

Away With Words

A is for amnesty which I donate my money to,
M is for the millions of people that are in jail today,
N is for nasty people that made me black and blue,
E is for everyone who can help in their own way,
S is for the safety that we all need,
T is for torture on which some governments feed,
Y is for you and the power of your words,
   Let us never be afraid to make our voices heard.

Siobhain Cahill (11)
Bryn Hafren Comprehensive School, Barry

Away With Words - For Prisoner Of Conscience, Helen Berhane

Why does this happen?
Why is it true?
I am in the prison,
Nothing to do.

Done nothing wrong,
I just sang a song,
I am really sad,
When I haven't done anything bad.

How can they expect me,
To give up my beliefs,
When I know God is with me,
Bringing comfort in my grief.

This metal box,
Is covered in locks,
I can hardly breathe,
I wish that I could leave.

Now it's dark,
I want to break this apart,
Get out this box,
Because I am really hot.

Now it's night,
I am going to fight,
I will be free
And I do believe.

I am Helen Berhane
And I will get out of this frame,
This will stop,
I will never be locked.

Lauren Gomes (11)
Bryn Hafren Comprehensive School, Barry

Away With Words

A little girl sat under a broken oak tree,
Away with all her words writing a poem was she,
She couldn't speak, so lonely, so cold,
She couldn't move against the wet dark mould.

A little girl sat in the cold winter night,
Feeling the chill in her anger and her fright,
A man came over and brought with him a bat,
To beat her to death as there alone she sat.

A little girl sat still while she was beaten in fear,
Everyone stared; screams are all they hear,
No one understands why this little girl was crushed,
As all her dreams have been blown away with the dust.

A little girl was lying under a broken oak tree,
With a poem in her hands, full of blood you could see,
The little girl breathed her last modest breath,
I'm sorry but this little girl's been beaten to death.

Lauren Avianne Tallemach (13)
Bryn Hafren Comprehensive School, Barry

Hallowe'en

A pitch-black night,
The moon is full,
Will they trick or treat?
I bet they will.

Nightmares of the dark,
Of the horror film monsters,
Blowing winds like chilling screams,
In the night the pumpkin festers.

Graveyards, ghosts and zombies,
Things that give me a fright,
Werewolves, bats and vampires,
Things that go *bump* in the night.

Charmaine Selwood (13)
Hartridge High School, Newport

Dad

R eady, steady, you're always there,
U always come when I am scared,
S o very loving, so very kind,
S o very furious when us, he can't find,
E ven though he knows we love him,
L oves us all when we're not with him,
L oving and caring, when messing with him.

He's the best!

Stacey Jones (11)
Hartridge High School, Newport

Football

F ootball is the game I love best,
O n the pitch you can't stop to have a rest,
O liver Khan kicks it out,
T he players run up and give it a clout,
B alls over the top to Theo Wallcott,
A s Rooney steps up to have a shot,
L isten to the fans as they roar,
L ook now, they've just scored.

Ryan O'Connor (12)
Hartridge High School, Newport

Basketball

B alling in the street with my homies,
A ll the people trying to stop the best baller from dunking,
S witching side to side like a flick knife,
K eep it cool and above the rim, like there's no strife,
E rupting like a mouse high jumper, so you couldn't stop him,
T all, skinny, muscly and strong, nothing will go wrong,
B alling is hard, but for the baller, it's not so much,
A ll the people cheering for him, but he is the one
    that will make the touch,
L owering the basketball as he is about to dunk,
L ife is always going to be full of punks.

Jamil Choudory (11)
Hartridge High School, Newport

Cars

Here we go racing around
And the crowd, they're standing around,
As the brilliant Michael Schumacher zooms around,
All the crowd were drinking beers,
As they roared with cheers,
Then as they try to overtake,
Faster than a baking steak,
Oh my goodness Michael Schumacher's crossed the line
And it's too late for the others to win,
Then one of the drivers gets thrown into a spin,
The people jump out of their skin.

Thomas Hill (11)
Hartridge High School, Newport

Dad

S trong when you pick me up,
T ired when you put me down,
E ven when I have had enough, he always tries again,
V ery funny, you make me laugh,
E very night, I kiss you goodnight,
N ever stop loving me.

T hat's because you're my daddy.

Yvonne Fleet (11)
Hartridge High School, Newport

Football

F ootball I think is the best,
O n the volley into their nest.
O n Gerrard's head, he flicks it on,
T erry smacks the ball, now it's gone.
B allack is running offside,
A s all the players run aside.
L evel now the scores are,
L iverpool cross and hit the bar.

Daniel Kiely (11)
Hartridge High School, Newport

Football

F riday lunchtime we kick about,
O ozing with sweat,
O out and about,
T ension building up,
B est performance by all,
A rmed with energy,
L egs crashing around,
L osing or winning, it is fun to play around.

Mahammed Adel Saad (13)
Hartridge High School, Newport

I'm Nothing

I'm sat here in a puddle of tears,
The sky is dark, I hope it clears,
All I wanted was a serenade,
Now I'm cutting myself with this blade,
You said you loved me, you're a liar,
Now my heart's suffocating with wire,
I can't talk now,
I'm gasping for breath,
Because I was heartbroken to death.

Now you're reading this suicide letter,
I'm nothing!
And it makes your life so much better.

Ryan Johnson (13)
Hartridge High School, Newport

Family

Some are normal,
Some are crazy,
They shout at you,
For being so lazy.
Up and out lazy bones,
The safest place
Is always at home,
After a long hard day
Of science and maths,
It's home I go to a nice warm bath,
Of love and affection,
The thing you get most is
A lot of protection,
They only want the best for you,
They give you lots of love,
My family means the most to me,
They are my prized possession,
I would not give them up,
For any worldly obsession,
I love them so much,
They mean so much to me,
There's Mum, Dad, my sister,
Nan and Grampy.

Jason Little (13)
Hartridge High School, Newport

Slugs

Slugs are small and slimy,
Squishy and squashy too,
All of them are yucky,
What are they meant to do?
They're only a big annoyance,
They only eat people's plants,
I think everyone would agree,
That we want them all gone!

Josh Poole (13)
Hartridge High School, Newport

Racism

Racism is as painful as a punch,
Racism is a form of bullying,
Racism could strike you,
Racism makes people feel low spirited,
People get bullied for the smallest things,
Like . . .
Colour,
Religion,
Appearance.

Racism is everywhere,
You can't hide it,
But you can stop it,
Stand up,
Speak up.

Daneka Cheshire (12)
Hartridge High School, Newport

Racism

Racism is totally wrong,
Stand up and be strong.

Prejudice is growing,
Stand up, speak up.

People thinking you're not kind,
Remember just put it behind.

Racism everywhere you go,
Town, shopping you never know.

The terrible taste of terror,
The painful punches.

Thomas Llewellyn (12)
Hartridge High School, Newport

My Worldwide Dreams

My dreams are full of wishes,
That may or may not come true,
I'd like to be an author
And illustrate my books.

Poverty for one,
Is such a terrible thing,
Please give money and food and stuff,
To stop that terrible thing.

Dreams may or may not come true,
Like being a teacher with little children,
Or being famous with my friends
And wearing all the coolest trends.

My dreams are full of wishes,
That may or may not come true,
To stop worldwide hunger,
Would be a wonderful thing to do.

Being rich doesn't mean a thing,
I'd like to be just in the middle,
Writing books and illustrating them,
Or being just in the middle.

Being poor isn't very nice
As long as we have some money each,
To buy the things we need,
For each and every day.

Francesca Morris (11)
Hartridge High School, Newport

Manchester United

Man Utd, Man Utd are the best,
They can beat all the rest,
They score one here, they score one there,
They're scoring goals everywhere,
Rooney, Ronaldo, Giggsy and the rest,
Ensure other teams are not the best.

Kieron Campbell (12)
Hartridge High School, Newport

My Car

We can race for cash,
But when I step on the gas,
My nitro goes blast,
My car is a Rover,
The engine turns over,
It tick-tocks like a clock,
Night and day I go out to pray for more cash,
I pick up my mates and go to Cardiff Gates,
To watch the match,
All these boys think they have good trims,
None of them can top my laser rims,
2 fast 2 furious, driving I go,
My car is my time to show.

Steven Taylor (13)
Hartridge High School, Newport

My World Dreams

I dream to be a designer,
Model my own clothes,
Wear them all over the world,
In the best fashion shows.

I want to be an actor,
I want to be a singer,
I want to go on TV
And most of all, X Factor.

I would like to be a gymnast,
Travel round the world,
I want be a famous person,
With many other girls.

I wish people wouldn't hurt animals and children,
By dumping animals,
Abusing children,
Going round to kill them.

So they're my dreams,
Now you see,
In the future,
What I want to be.

Jamie Warner (11)
Hartridge High School, Newport

My Dream

My name is Jacob and my dream is to . . .
Stop cruelty and sexual abuse, let's bring joy to the world,
I dream of being an actor and pleasing the spectator,
Yet again I hope nobody ruins it.

I want world peace, freedom from pollution,
I want love and happiness to break free,
I wish to live in a luxurious castle,
I want to always have fun and never be bored.

I want a beautiful wife with plenty of money,
I want to live in harmony just like an angel,
I wish to be rich and famous,
But over all, it really doesn't matter.

Jacob Huish
Hartridge High School, Newport

My Dreams

My dreams are to become a cartoon drawer
And make up my own toons
And design clothes,
To see in fashion shows,
I dream to have pets,
That never go to the vets.

My world dreams would be to have world war gone
And replaced with world peace,
Give all hungry kids as much as they can eat.

Kayleigh Poole (11)
Hartridge High School, Newport

Football

Football, football is the best,
Better than all the rest,
Shooting, tackling, volleying and passing,
Until the whistle goes,
Everyone stands on their toes,
Yellow cards, you have one more chance,
Red card, you're going off,
The goalkeeper is concentrating,
So don't disturb him,
The crowd is going wild,
None of them have a child.

Bethan Spruce (12)
Hartridge High School, Newport

Monsters

M onsters hiding under my bed,
O n my tongue words can't be said,
N oises going through my head,
S taying still I think they're dead,
T ossing and turning in my bed,
E arache, backache and headache instead,
R unning pins and needles going through my thumb,
S illy me, it's just my mum.

Chanice Edwards (11)
Hartridge High School, Newport

Racism Is Not Right

Racism is definitely not right,
You should always put up a fight,
Walking through the streets,
People looking at your feet
And thinking in their minds,
You're one of those black kind,
People walking through the dark
And thinking oh my God he's dark,
Racism, racism, it's not right,
Don't give up without a fight.

Jamie Derrick (12)
Hartridge High School, Newport

Tropical Imagination

The sky is blue,
The sea is calm,
All on this island on which I am,
The stream is flowing because something's glowing.

The ocean matching the deep blue sky
Passion fruit falling from way up high,
What a beautiful feeling from the sky,
The noise of streams flowing ahead.

Fishes are splashed in their bed,
Water so clear and fruit so fine,
This feeling is so divine,
I love this island which is mine.

The birds are tweeting for their young,
Frogs are glowing from fireflies,
Which they've gummed . . .
The teacher calls me, I'm back in class,
I will never forget that land of mine.

Taher Mansfield (11)
Hartridge High School, Newport

Dreams!

D azzling dreams,
R eally exciting dreams,
E xquisite dreams,
A mazing dreams,
M ind-blowing dreams,
S weet, soft dreams.

Paige Jones (12)
Hartridge High School, Newport

Football

Football, football away we go,
Gerrard gets injured and breaks his toe,
The stretchers come on and realise it's a con,
The crowd start singing the 'con' song,
Talking loudly, Benitez shouts,
It's not long now before he goes out,
Scouser Steven gives it a clout,
He scores and everyone shouts.

Nikita Evans (11)
Hartridge High School, Newport

I Wish

I wish I could
Stop world hunger
And to solve cruelty to animals
It's true people are.

I'd love to be a designer
With all the best clothes
'Cause I would make them myself
That would be amazing.

I dream that I can
Give peace to the world
Instead of all these wars
We all just got along.

I want to be a model
Strutting down the catwalk
Tossing and turning
All around the world.

Kirsty Knorz (12)
Hartridge High School, Newport

My Dream

I wish I was a model,
Standing and walking,
Turning around,
Nice and pretty.

I wish I was a designer,
I could design my own clothes,
I could stitch until I was dead,
I would be very popular.

My dream is to be a netball player,
Win for my team,
I would be very popular,
Don't you think.

My dream is to be a pop star,
I would go to London screaming my socks off,
Dancing with the floor and singing.

My dream for the world,
Is to stop cruelty to children,
Stop dumping the animals
And to have world peace.

Bethan Clayton (11)
Hartridge High School, Newport

Monsters

Monsters big, monsters small, monsters young, monsters old,
Monsters sleeping under my bed,
With me looking overhead,
Wait until morning rises,
Then you'll get a big surprise,
My mum comes to wake me up and gets a big shock,
As I'm shaking in my frock.

Tammarah Fowler (11)
Hartridge High School, Newport

My Little Sister Anya

My little sister Anya is angelic as can be,
With her head full of curls, she's nothing like me,
Great big blue eyes which sparkle and shine,
She likes to have fun and makes me laugh all the time.

When I come home from school, she's always there,
For a kiss and a cuddle like a small teddy bear,
At night-time when I go to sleep,
Anya's the last thing that leaves my busy head.

Ellesse Buss (13)
Hartridge High School, Newport

My Pet Dragon

I have a pet dragon, that no one has seen,
He lives squashed under my bed, where no one has been,
I had my pet dragon when I was just four,.
It was a bitter night, as he just waltzed through my front door,
My dragon is immense, he has purple and white spots,
But when he gets mad, he has black and blue dots,
He's a lazy old fart, he never helps me round the house,
He just sits on the sofa and watches Mickey Mouse,
He burns holes in my clothes and wakes me up with his sloppy chops
And he blows me away with his whirlwind coughs,
But that's my imaginary dragon that lives inside my head,
That no one has seen because he sleeps under my bed.

Alex O'Neill (13)
Hartridge High School, Newport

Kick-Boxing

Kickboxing is a sport I do,
Every night at quarter to,
In the centre we kick and punch,
Then go home and have some lunch,
Sometimes we do sparring sessions,
Which is good for us because it takes up half the lesson,
Warming up is a thing we do,
Keeping the muscles as good as new,
Keeping quiet is a thing we do more,
Otherwise you'll be out the door,
The teacher would say get in a press-up position,
Until he makes his decision,
As soon as the teacher leaves the door,
Everyone gets up and does no more,
When the teacher comes back through the door,
Everyone gets up and does even more,
After about 10 minutes or so,
The teacher will say, 'Sparring gear on, c'mon let's go!'
Then everyone will put on their sparring kit,
Some people don't like it and have a fit,
At the end of the class we do a solution,
Then I go home and use the PlayStation.

Benjamin Shatford (13)
Hartridge High School, Newport

Christmas Poem

Families celebrate this time of year,
With Christmas trees, tinsel and loads, loads more,
They wait in their beds, snuggled and warm,
Waiting for Santa to come through the door,
Then when the morning comes, they go downstairs,
Hoping that Santa has visited them again,
They open the door with their feet on the floor,
They jump in amazement with smiles on their faces,
Then later in the day, they all sit down,
They pull their crackers and put on their crowns,
With snow outside and people singing,
With lights and trees that flicker at night,
They maybe give you a fright
And they go to bed, snuggled and warm,
Wishing that Christmas would be here again.

Matthew Kerslake (13)
Hartridge High School, Newport

The Girl That Beat Her Step-Mum

Sit back and listen to my song,
'Bout a girl who beat her step-mum,
A pop princess named Ebony,
She had a jealous step-mummy,
This mum owned a cool MP3,
But she wouldn't listen to Ebony,
That step-mum released some pop,
To try and knock Ebony off the top,
This made the girl sound like a minger,
But soon she met and joined 7 backing singers,
Back up went Ebony Rose,
Her mum just stuck up her nose,
Two wicked platinum's later,
Mum made a band called 'Nater,'
Down Ebony went again,
This time sounding more than lame,
After a while of hide-and-seek,
Ebony reached her highest peak,
Her step-mum was so fed up,
That she went after Ebony with a poisoned cup,
Ebony wouldn't have the drink
But started to sing her new song called 'Chink'
The step-mum tried to sing,
But then her voice went with a *ping*
The pop princess ruled the charts
And her wicked step-mum cleaned out carts,
It's now the end of my song,
'Bout a girl who beat her step-mum.

Harriet Smith (13)
Hartridge High School, Newport

History

H istory is great!
I n times when I've little to do,
S tories from the past give me a clue,
T ime goes past very fast and
O rders from the past affect us at last,
R aging from the time the telephone rang,
Y et even to the year that Elvis first sang!

I s it the best lesson of them all, *yes!*
S o let's begin and learn some more.

G reat people from the past saw time go past,
R eally really fast,
E lizabethan ships with tall high mast, sailed to America using maps
A nd man discovered and brought back slaves dressed in scraps,
T o come to the end of the poem, history is the best lesson going!

Charlie Ford (12)
Hartridge High School, Newport

Netball

Netball, netball is my hobby,
Passing and shooting,
Winning, never losing,
Playing home, playing away,
This will be our final day,
Training, training, all day long,
When it hits 4 o'clock, I'll be
Gone!

Rebecca Bill (13)
Hartridge High School, Newport

Spiders, Spiders

Spiders, spiders everywhere I look,
Red glowing eyes and black fluffy legs,
I hate them, I hate them,
What do I do?
Spiders, spiders on the wall.

Spiders, spiders crawling on me,
Help me! Help me!
I want to kill them all.

Hannah Shingler (12)
Hartridge High School, Newport

Friends

Friends are special,
They tell you everything,
Never pass off a friend,
They're always there,
When you need them,
Never be horrible to a friend,
They never tell your secrets,
Never worry about a friend,
A true friend will always be there for you.

Megan Bliss (12)
Hartridge High School, Newport

Man United

M an United are the best,
A lways better than the rest,
N ever losing.

U nited as one they beat all,
N ever greedy,
I nvincible on the ball,
T riple holders,
E ver winning,
D ouble winners.

Andrew Wright (12)
Hartridge High School, Newport

Running

Running, running so fast,
You'll never see me coming last,
All the people in the crowd,
Screaming and shouting nice and loud.

Training at clubs after school,
I think it's really cool,
Hearing the gun at the beginning of a race,
You've got to run fast, but keep a pace.

Running, running down the lane,
Both your legs are in pain,
Coming to the end of the race,
Don't slow down and still keep a pace.

Hollie Short (13)
Hartridge High School, Newport

Lonely

Lonely in the school yard,
Only one around,
Nobody to talk to,
Empty of all friends,
Lonely in the school yard,
Yelling in my head,
Waiting for the bell to go,
Watching everyone with friends.

Benjamin Jones (12)
Hartridge High School, Newport

Dancing In London Was So Fab

D ancing is great,
A ll my friends go,
N o nasty people ever show,
C all all the dancers,
I n her majesties we are,
N othing but tapping,
G iggling and laughing.

I n Planet Hollywood our
N ames, we're on the board.

L ondon we have danced,
O vernight we stayed,
N othing but claps,
D ancing is so fab,
O ver and over people still clapped,
N othing but dancing we do.

W illing to do it,
A ll ready and prepared,
S inging, dancing, everything was there.

S elling programmes, some people were,
O n and off within 3 minutes.

F antastic the
A udience were, they even,
B egan to scream because we were so fab,
All thanks to our teacher,
Vanessa Clarke!

Mandy Harvey (12)
Hartridge High School, Newport

Racism

Racism is painful,
People might act differently on the outside,
But on the inside we're all the same,
The fear fights you for freedom,
Piercing lifeless eyes.

People give you daggers in your glittering eyes,
The smell of fear,
Segregation is heartless,
Prejudice is spiteful.

What's the point?

Emily Campbell (12)
Hartridge High School, Newport

Racism

Racism hurts like a blow to the head,
It's as cruel and as mean as a thunderstorm,
Their evil minds and glaring eyes,
Pain is only smelt and brought by the heartless.

It makes people feel as lonely as an abandoned puppy,
It's pointless and shouldn't be done,
It's prejudging people by the way they look or speak,
It makes people feel sick to even watch it.

It's horrible to think how many people do it,
To hear it happening every day,
To see the tears in their eyes,
To hear them cry and scream,
Someone should help them,
Maybe it could be you!

Rhiannon Elizabeth Tucker (12)
Hartridge High School, Newport

Racism

Discrimination is wrong,
Can't we all be happy
And sing a merry song?

Black, white everywhere,
In my dream I can't bear,
At the end of the day,
Can we all get along and share?

Be happy, be free,
Don't say a word, just break free.

New baby boys,
New baby girls,
All different colours around the world.

Stand up, speak up,
Break free, it's your dream.

Elicia Collins (12)
Hartridge High School, Newport

Racism

Destroyed lives retaliate,
Immunity is what they fought for,
Immunity is what they got,
They did not give up their vision.

Anger filled the world,
Anger is in their eyes,
They are waiting for a reaction
And also satisfaction.

Racism is wrong,
They should all stay strong,
It's not kind,
So leave it behind,
In the back of your mind.

Josh Allsopp (12)
Hartridge High School, Newport

Racism

The eyes are piercing and cold,
He laughs at everyone that's black,
Racism doesn't get you friends,
Segregation is wrong,
Stand up, speak up for freedom,
The words hit you like a ton of bricks,
It scars them for life,
Crying goes on and on,
Martin Luther King, Malcolm X they're gone,
They were black and they were assassinated,
The list is never-ending,
So fight for what is right,
Don't use chants and curses,
Use nice words, be friends not enemies.

Daniel Dervin (12)
Hartridge High School, Newport

Racism

Living in freedom,
Everyone should be free,
Racism is wrong,
It hurts people's feelings,
In my eyes,
Colour shouldn't matter,
Everybody is the same.

People are violent
And racist,
Racism should stop,
There are consequences,
So stop!

Shadine Evans (12)
Hartridge High School, Newport

Racism

Racism is wrong,
Different treatment because of colour,
Discrimination,
Labelling the sound of horror,
Slavery is touched once again,
Power strikes out,
Look inside their eyes and find greed,
Out of control,
People judged on their religion and beliefs,
Stereotype,
The taste of racist words,
Hatred because of love and beauty,
Stand up, speak up.

Natalie Bevan (13)
Hartridge High School, Newport

What's The Point?

The glare of evilness in their eyes,
What's the point?
The rush of strikes from their fists,
What's the point?
The words of hate from their mouths,
What's the point?
Racism,
What's the point?

James Pitt (12)
Hartridge High School, Newport

Racism Is Mean

Racism is mean,
I wish it was all a bad dream,
Hatred is horrible,
Fearful eyes afraid of fear,
Bullies should be bullied,
Black people are just the same,
But a different colour,
Prejudice is wrong,
Discrimination should just be a song,
Racism is mean,
I wish it was all a bad dream.

Hannah Bishop (12)
Hartridge High School, Newport

Racism Poem

Walking through the street,
With no one you know to meet,
Eyes stare and glare,
No one who cares,
Darker skin,
Evil grin,
Cuts and bruises,
Dark people loses,
Living in fear,
Shedding a tear,
Cruel souls,
Deep holes,
Cold eyes,
Their happiness dies.

Kayleigh Lewis (13)
Hartridge High School, Newport

Racism

Racism is nasty and spiteful,
Calling people black, white,
That's not right.

Segregation

Malicious men, frightful women,
Racism is horror, it's in houses
And in the streets.

Bullied for being black,
Bullied for being white,
Why is this still happening,
When we know it's not right?

Discrimination

Black and white, white and black,
The colour of our skin doesn't match,
So what?

Seana O'Driscoll (12)
Hartridge High School, Newport

My Dream

I dream for world peace, and harmony
And to stop hunger and devastation,
I dream to stop child abuse and animal abuse
And to help people in need,
I dream to stop wars and arguments
And to make the world a better place.

My wishes are to maybe be an artist
And travel all over the world!
I would do sketchings and drawings
And lots of paintings,
That's what I'd like to do.

I would also like to look after animals
And cure then when they're sick,
I'd make sure they get good homes
And save all kinds of species.

Hannah Giles (12)
Hartridge High School, Newport

Sisters

We scream and fight,
Morning to night,
We laugh, we cry,
We make time fly,
I ask for things and she says 'No!'
Mum is downstairs saying she wants to go.

Maybe it's true we love each other,
But, sometimes I think I'd rather it was
Me and Mother.

Ashleigh Lloyd
Hartridge High School, Newport

Winter

W hy does ice start to fall?
I want to know it all,
N ot to play out or in,
T o show it the sting of the winter ice,
E arly in the morning Santa calls, with snowflakes cold and all
R ighteous snow continues to fall, ice and all.

W hy does ice start to fall?
A ll in cold and all,
T ouch the great cold of ice,
E lectric sting from freeze of night,
R ight to say the sun draws near to show us its burning fear.

Callum Tufft (11)
Hartridge High School, Newport

Hallowe'en Horror

Spooky and scary,
Dark and cold,
Don't you love Hallowe'en,
Hallowe'en is gold,
Sweets and tricks,
Isn't it gold,
Don't you just love Hallowe'en?
It never gets old.

Aimee Rees (12)
Hartridge High School, Newport

Rugby

R unning down the great big pitch,
U nder pressure, there's always a glitch,
G randstand close, don't turn away!
B oys and girls come to watch us play,
Y oung or old, it doesn't matter if you want to have fun
And play, just come and join in the game.

Joshua Stock
Hartridge High School, Newport

Cars

C ars are really cool, whoever hates them is a fool
A nd I take my friends to the pub to play a game of pool,
R acing cars, fast cars, they all really rule,
S itting down in the front car seat thinking it's a dream.
 But I am driving a racing car now and not in school.

Leighton Phillips
Hartridge High School, Newport

Football Friends

I love football,
Football loves me,
The way I kick,
It likes to flick,
When I score,
The crowd roar,
When I defend,
The ball's not my friend,
When they score,
I have to ignore!
When I take kick-off,
The players race off
And we all love football.

Joshua Sweet (11)
Hartridge High School, Newport

Trick Or Treat

I go out at night,
To put people in for a fright,
They scream and shout,
When my tongue pokes out,
I say, 'Trick or treat?'
They give me something to eat,
Now it's time to eat some sweets,
As I had fun going trick or treat.

Shannon Trigg (11)
Hartridge High School, Newport

My Poem On Animals

Animals are funny, some act like monkeys,
Some like the cold, some like the warm,
I like animals,
I hope you do too,
Come on, animals love you.

Animals are slow when they eat too much,
Especially pandas with bamboo,
Animals are cool,
I know they don't look like it,
But when you get to know them,
You will love them too.

Animals love you, I hope you love them too?
Because some people give them abuse,
I know some people sneeze around them,
But you can still love them,
Animals love you, why can't you love them too?

Louise Tamplin (11)
Hartridge High School, Newport

Girls Are About . . .

Flip-flops, belly tops,
Short skirts, love to flirt,
Lemonade in the shade,
Blue skies, hot guys,
Late nights, water fights,
Ice creams, sweet dreams,
Party time, looking fine,
Sleeping in, sneaking out,
That's what us girls are all about!

Bonnie Arlett (12)
Hartridge High School, Newport

Friends

Friends are people that cheer you up,
When you're down,
Friends are people you spend
All your time with.

Georgina is amazing,
Great, fun and bubbly,
When I'm down she's always around,
She's like a bouncy ball.

Megan is fantastic,
Marvellous, mad and kind,
When I'm alone, she's never far,
She's like a magic wizard.

Bethan is great,
Brilliant, brainy and funny,
When I'm with her,
It's always fun,
She's like a film star.

Ellie is brilliant,
Excellent, funny and weird,
When I'm in fear,
She's always near,
She's like a helium balloon.

All my friends are ace,
I couldn't ask for more.

Natalie West (13)
Hartridge High School, Newport

Away With Words

On the 15th of August we were born,
Not in the afternoon, but in the morn,
First it was my brother, then it was me,
We both arrived at 10 past 3,
When we grew up, we loved each other
And also our Dad and our Mother,
On the 17th June, somebody broke my heart,
As my brother and I were to part,
I know my brother was only 7,
But I know he's so happy now in Heaven,
As he plays in Heaven with all the doves,
All I want to do is send him my love.

Jessica Evans (12)
Hartridge High School, Newport

Away With Words

Football, football is the best,
Football, football will beat the rest,
Football, football is like the Earth,
When we play on the Astro Turf.

Football, football is number one,
Running, kicking, having fun,
Football, football, join the team,
Football, football, you've got to scream.

Football, football, can you see what I mean?
Don't play dirty, please play clean,
Listen to me well and listen to me good,
You'll love football, I know you could.

Football, football is the best,
Football, football will beat the rest.

Leigh Derrick (12)
Hartridge High School, Newport

Christmas!

Christmas is a fine time of year,
Everybody drinks wine and beer,
It's just that happy time of year,
Where everyone likes a good old cheer.

Presents, presents all around,
Some of them are on the ground,
Some of them are really big,
To find the best, you need to dig.

Christmas trees are all lit up,
But that's not good if you have a pup,
You often find stars on top,
After you've bought them from the shop.

Christmas dinners are really nice,
Especially ones with a little spice,
Turkey, carrots are just like lunch,
Even better than some brunch.

Mark O'Connell (12)
Hartridge High School, Newport

Untitled

A ll things bright and beautiful,
M ay they all rule the world,
Y ou will see the change in the world and in you too!

M ay all the animals live happy
A nd with enough food and drink,
N ature is part of life,
S mall and big animals, enough room for all,
F at and thin animals may rest in peace,
I nner peace for all kinds of animals,
E nemies should help animals to survive,
L earn and listen in school so you could help save animals,
D rink and food, may be needed for support.

Amy Mansfield (13)
Hartridge High School, Newport

Stay Healthy

Veggies, veggies good for your bones,
You cannot eat stuff like stones,
You like chicken and chips,
Don't worry, that's OK,
But you do have to pay it off some day.

You do like cheese,
Eat up those peas,
Your veggies keep you good,
Come be healthy, you know you could.

Eat healthy and be fit
And can wear that old football kit,
Come on, be healthy and fit,
Go on, try on your football kit.

Kirsty Louise Willis (11)
Hartridge High School, Newport

My Dog Kiara

My dog Kiara is a lab
And I'd say she's blooming fab,
Her fur is as black as the darkest night,
Her eyes are really bright,
She really is a delight.

Her coat is as shiny as a newly polished shoe,
Her little sister Dolla came from the zoo,
Her tail wags around the clock,
I didn't shout when she ate my sock,
I took her to the vets when she got sick,
When I get home, she gives me a lick.

Sometimes it's like she talks,
Especially when it's time for walks,
Her favourite game is chasing a ball
And even though you might say she's small,
In my eyes, she's the best of them all.

Shawn James (12)
Hartridge High School, Newport

The Greatest Team

Arsenal is the greatest team,
Passing, scoring always seen,
Arsenal has the best players,
As best as you can get,
No team can beat them,
Maybe sometimes, just not yet,
Arsenal is kind of like Brazil,
Showing off with all their skill,
Arsenal score nearly every match,
Players shoot, our keepers will catch,
When the ref blows his whistle at the end of the game,
Arsenal still stay the same,
Whatever the score is, win 2-0 or lose 2-0,
Arsenal is still brill,
Arsenal is just the greatest team.

Liam Codd (12)
Hartridge High School, Newport

Away With Words

Hockey is my favourite sport,
I play it every week,
Players passing perfectly across the premier pitch,
There you can hear the clank of the hockey sticks,
Running up and down the wing,
Looking when to switch,
As I dribble in and out,
My hockey stick glides about,
As I lunge at the ball,
As quick as a flash,
I am stopped by somebody tall,
As I run back and forth,
I like to strike and make a score,
If the game I played is lost,
I do not lose my head,
But if the game is a magnificent win,
I stand there with a huge big grin.

Matthew Tucker (12)
Hartridge High School, Newport

My First Day At School

My first day at school,
I was shaking like a leaf,
My head all over the place,
Counting the number of feet,
Put in rooms with loads of faces,
Made me feel I was in different places.

I met this one girl called Leanne,
She looked a bit pickled,
She asked me if I needed help,
With my times table,
Also helped me in maths,
In Miss Wilkie's class.

At the end of the day,
I walked home alone,
Seeing if I could see,
Anyone I knew,
Until the next day I never knew,
What wouldl happen to me soon.

Vicki-Marie Richardson (12)
Hartridge High School, Newport

Hallowe'en

It is once again that time of year,
Where kids dress up and shout and cheer,
Knocking on doors to trick or treat,
Friends, neighbours and strangers they meet.

The costumes look scary and give you a fright,
As witches and ghosts run into the night,
Others as werewolves with lots of drool,
Keep your eyes open, you may see a ghoul.

In the murky, miserable middle of the night,
Oh it is a super and shocking sight,
To see the horrible creatures creep,
It's enough to make you wish you were asleep.

As real life zombies with faces white as chalk,
Murmuring and moaning as they shuffle and walk,
Back to their graves whilst day draws near,
Asking each other, 'Have you see my ear?'

Vampires and mummies all wrapped up in tape,
As the cats of the witches try to make their escape,
But as the witches zoom off and fly,
I guess it is time to say my goodbye.

Oliver Griffiths (12)
Hartridge High School, Newport

My Chocolate Lab

Archie is my chocolate lab,
He really makes me smile,
He jumps about all the time
And usually walks a mile.

His paws are soft,
His eyes are brown,
He's the most
Beautiful dog in town.

Anything and everything,
My greedy dog will eat,
Carrots, grass, wood,
Shoes, biscuits or meat.

He really is the perfect dog,
He makes me very proud,
He is the most amazing friend,
He stands out in a crowd.

Paige Attewell (13)
Hartridge High School, Newport

Romans

The ancient people of Rome,
They conquered as far as the eye could see,
North, south, east and west,
The Romans had it all.

The empire of Rome,
Spread far and wide,
The emperor decapitated anyone who opposed.

Their armies strong,
Their inventions bold,
Their stories are old,
But still being told.

Ancient Rome,
Ancient yet . . .
Still being found.

Zak Yearsley (13)
Hartridge High School, Newport

Hallowe'en

Ghouls and ghosts swimming through the sky,
Witches glaring at you eye to eye,
Scary noises bump in the night,
Watch out, the vampire bats do bite!

Pull the bed sheets up to your chin,
Because the Hallowe'en fun is about to begin,
Don't close your eyes or rest your head,
The bogeyman is under the bed.

Zombies, at midnight, rise out of their tombs,
Thick fog and evil seem to loom,
Skeletons jiggle and rattle their bones,
The werewolves are howling and the mummies do groan.

Banshees screaming in the dead of night,
Goblins and pixies begin to fight,
Warlocks conjuring magic spells,
Let's hope tonight all goes well.

Chelsea Toms (12)
Hartridge High School, Newport

Fire

Warm as fire,
Hot as coal,
A new shadow crept in,
Through the hole,
A voice speaks from behind,
A face looking, is it in my mind?
A man with problems,
I will need help,
A girl with love,
So hot it melts,
It's real bad when you feel down,
Just pick up a book and
Write it all down.

Carysann Fowler (12)
Hartridge High School, Newport

Wrongness Of Racism

Racism is savage,
It is a reign of power,
Some people are sobbing in slavery,
It is a form of bullying.

Do not judge people,
They are the same as us,
Some people are as spiteful towards them.

The taste of fear,
In their faces
And the glint in their eyes,
The smell of hatred,
Racism is wrong,
So make it stop!

Ryan Everett (12)
Hartridge High School, Newport

Put Up A Fight!

Racism is sickening,
Whether it's skin or hair,
What the hell,
Who cares?

People think racism
Hurts feelings but it
Doesn't, it hurts your
Soul and can sometimes
Kill.

Whether someone's black
Or someone's white,
There's no point in
Arguing or fighting.

We can put an end
To racism, we just
Have to put
Up a fight!

Ashley Edmunds (12)
Hartridge High School, Newport

I'd Rather Be

I'd rather be thin than fat,
I'd rather be a dog than a cat,
I'd rather be a cap than a hat,
I'd rather be a carpet than a mat,
I'd rather be a house than a flat,
I'd rather be a flea than a gnat,
I'd rather be stood than sat,
I'd rather be a bird than a bat,
I'd rather be a mouse than a rat,
I'd rather be me than Pat!

Luke Retout (13)
Ruthin School, Ruthin

I'd Rather Be

I'd rather be a cat than a dog,
I'd rather be a toad than a frog,
I'd rather kiss than snog,
I'd rather be coal than a log,
I'd rather be a saw than a hog,
I'd rather be a toilet than a bog,
I'd rather be a wheel than a cog,
I'd rather be snow than fog,
I'd rather run than jog,
I'd rather be ten than fifteen tog.

Adam Roberts (13)
Ruthin School, Ruthin

I'd Rather Be

I'd rather be a dog than a cat,
I'd rather be a mouse than a rat,
I'd rather be a rug than a mat,
I'd rather be a fly than a gnat,
I'd rather be Betty than Pat,
I'd rather be a glove than a hat,
I'd rather be thin than fat,
I'd rather be a house than a flat,
I'd rather be silent than chat,
I'd rather be this than that,
I'd rather be posh than tat,
I'd rather be a splodge than a splat,
I'd rather be stood than sat,
I'd rather be good than a brat.

Charlotte Baugh (12)
Ruthin School, Ruthin

I'd Rather Be

I'd rather be a basket than a bin,
I'd rather be beer than gin,
I'd rather have legs than a fin,
I'd rather be out than in,
I'd rather be fat than thin,
I'd rather be gold than tin,
I'd rather be good than sin,
I'd rather be me than Bryn,
I'd rather be yang than yin,
I'd rather be an apple than a mandarin,
I'd rather be a pencil than a pen,
I'd rather lose than win,
I'd rather be a hotel than an inn,
I'd rather be a knee than a shin,
I'd rather have eyes than a chin,
I'd rather be a drum than a mandolin,
I'd rather be a guitar than a violin,
I'd rather be friends than kin,
I'd rather be china than porcelain,
I'd rather be in Chester than Ruthin,
I'd rather be Ashley than Quentin.

Ashley Griffiths (13)
Ruthin School, Ruthin

Sonnet

I love horse riding very much, but why?
I always like to be around horses,
It makes me laugh and smile and cry,
I love to complete horse riding courses.

When I ride I am content and happy,
I spend my days at the riding stables,
If you went horse riding, then you would see,
Try it for a while, you're more than able.

Riding means more than to sit on a horse,
Then there is more when you get off also,
There's a lot to do especially chores,
You do a lot of running to and fro.

Whether it's in the field or on the yard,
It's always fun but challengingly hard.

Ellie Birkett (11)
Ruthin School, Ruthin

I'd Rather Be

I'd rather be red than blue,
I'd rather be him not you,
I'd rather be tape not glue,
I'd even be Sam not Hugh,
I'd rather be called Sue than Lou,
I'd rather swallow not chew,
I'd rather be old than new,
I'd rather be more than few,
I'd rather be sick than have flu,
I'd rather be what not who,
I'd rather be a boot than a shoe,
I'd rather have a toilet than a loo.

Dafydd Atkinson (13)
Ruthin School, Ruthin

A Letter Back Home

The sun scorched the open plains,
Of where I lived,
In olden days.

Now I flee from that country,
To seek asylum,
For my safety.

The government was harsh and rash,
We worked and worked,
For Western cash.

I arrive in England and now head west,
With no money,
To protest!

These Western folk don't understand,
That their government,
Ruins our land.

I miss my home country, it's true,
But here I am,
To fight for you!

Catherine Jones
Ruthin School, Ruthin

I'd Rather Be

I'd rather be a queen than a king,
I'd rather be swimming than skipping,
I'd rather be diamonds than bling,
I'd rather be porcelain than ming,
I'd rather be something than nothing,
I'd rather bong than bing,
I'd rather be yang than ying,
I'd rather be a necklace than a ring,
I'd rather act than sing,
I'd rather have a tail than a wing,
I'd rather be cool than amazing,
I'd rather be funny than boring,
I'd rather be a key than a keyring,
I'd rather be a floor than a ceiling,
I'd rather have money for shopping,
I'd rather be healed than healing.

Lorna Elizabeth Drake (13)
Ruthin School, Ruthin

The Hunt

It's time to start the hunt,
To destroy the beast,
Stop it killing our livestock,
It all goes quiet,
Everything is still,
A dart of red and orange,
Jumps out,
Blow loud the bugle,
The chase begins,
Through the trees,
Over fences,
The horses jump,
The hounds bark,
The chase is long,
Finally they make their kill.

Lara Pritchard (13)
Ruthin School, Ruthin

Swimming Club

What happens when I go to swimming club,
So many swimming galas make me wise,
Even though I might end up as a sub,
But then I might end up with butterflies.

Front crawl is one of my favourite strokes,
Although butterfly is one of them too!
But other people may need a quick poke,
What happens when I get the dreaded flu?

Swimming breaststroke is extremely hard,
Perhaps one day I might pick up some pace,
I will get a congratulation's card
And then I might just win a breaststroke race!

When I finish swimming at swimming club,
The water from the pool drains down the plug!

Alexander Dowell (11)
Ruthin School, Ruthin

Sonnet

Are Arsenal better than Liverpool?
Of course it can never be true to say,
Anyone who thinks so must be a fool,
Reds always win at the end of the day,
Glory, glory for Liverpool heroes,
Returning so thrilled to Anfield, their home,
Arsenal defeated the Gunners were foes,
Returning to Highbury to cry alone,
Liverpool have a wide range of players,
Reina is Spanish and Kromkamp is Dutch,
Gerrard is one of the top, great players,
I think Liverpool love scoring so much,
Liverpool are better than Arsenal,
I think Arsenal are really dull.

Robin Pritchard (11)
Ruthin School, Ruthin

Sonnet

MUFC why do you play so well?
You won the treble in 1999,
It was a great game, it was so swell,
You're so great, so fine, I wish you were mine,
Rooney and Ronaldo, such great players,
Scholes and Carrick are strong in midfield,
Sir Alex Ferguson, should be the next mayor,
The defence is like a rock, like a shield,
The crowd in the Stretford End sing so loud,
We sing all the songs, we never stop singing,
When we're singing, in the sky not a cloud,
The look on the scousers' faces when we win is minging,
We have legends like Cantona and George Best,
We score goals like it's a scoring fest.

George De Vera Davey (11)
Ruthin School, Ruthin

I'd Rather Be

I'd rather be thin than fat,
I'd rather be a dog than a cat,
I'd rather be a house than a flat,
I'd rather be a floor than a mat,
I'd rather be clever than a prat,
I'd rather be me than Pat,
I'd rather be stood than sat,
I'd rather be a mouse than a bat.

Ashley Burrows Brown (12)
Ruthin School, Ruthin

I'd Rather Be

I'd rather be a dog than a cat,
I'd rather be a shoe than a mat,
I'd rather be thin than fat,
I'd rather be a cake than a rat,
I'd rather wear silver than tat,
I'd rather giggle than chat,
I'd rather be called Claire than Pat,
I'd rather wear a bandanna than a hat.

Holly Morris (12)
Ruthin School, Ruthin

I'd Rather Be

I'd rather be a tree than a log,
I'd rather be a horse than a hog,
I'd rather be a man than a dog,
I'd rather say 'har' than 'og',
I'd rather be smoke than smog,
I'd rather be tassel than tog,
I'd rather be a wood than a bog,
I'd rather be loved than snog,
I'd rather be clag than clog,
I'd rather be a wheel than a cog,
I'd rather be dry than sog,
I'd rather be a cloud than fog,
I'd rather be sold than flog,
I'd rather be kick than slog,
I'd rather be animal than zog,
I'd rather play snatch, than pog,
I'd rather walk than jog,
I'd rather be zog than quog,
I'd rather wear specs than gog.

Ruairidh Kerrigan (12)
Ruthin School, Ruthin

The Magic Box
(Based on 'Magic Box' by Kit Wright)

I will put in my box . . .

The skin of a snake,
Th sound of an earthquake,
The taste of a birthday cake.

I will put in my box . . .

The soft snow settling,
The texture of a white cloud,
The roar of the untamed ocean.

I will put in my box . . .

The twinkle of a shining star,
Soft sand from the Caribbean,
The rustle of the leaves.

I will put in my box . . .

The spring of a leaping frog,
The whistle of the whistling wind,
The sound of a heartbeat.

My box is different from pain
To gain, to glory.

I shall hear the roar of the crowd,
As the kettle is ready to pour.

Robert Jones (12)
St Gerard's School Trust, Bangor

My Magic Box
(Based on 'Magic Box' by Kit Wright)

I will put in my box . . .

A language not yet spoken,
A spell not yet discovered
And a tree that grows pure gold.

I will put in my box . . .

Words spoken from a dolphin,
A smile from the sun
And the tear shed by a cloud.

I will put in my box . . .

Memories of my childhood,
An animal that was years ago extinct
And the poisonous apple eaten by Adam.

I will put in my box . . .

The prettiest of all the angel wings,
The most magical and powerful fairy dust
And the most gorgeous horn of a unicorn.

My box is fashioned from glitter and crystals,
With rubies on the lid and pure gold in the corners,
Its hinges are the toe joints of dinosaurs.

I shall dance in my box,
In the great hall of a castle I built
And we'll dance away till the sun shall rise.

Amber Langford (12)
St Gerard's School Trust, Bangor

My Magic Box
(Based on 'Magic Box' by Kit Wright)

I will put in my box . . .

A trumpet of twenty elephants,
The smell of rain after a drought,
The sight of a cheetah getting ready to pounce.

I will put in my box . . .

The smell of the African plain,
A newborn giraffe trying to stand on its wobbly legs,
A meerkat pup on its first day out of the burrow.

I will put in my box . . .

The snap of a crocodile's jaws as it
Unsuccessfully tries to catch its prey,
The whinny of a terrified zebra,
The beauty of a newborn elephant calf.

My box is fashioned out of strong yellow grass,
In each corner there is an African tribal song,
My box is protected by a long-forgotten curse.

I shall ride elephants and race cheetahs
And sing with the African tribes in my box,
Then sizzle in the hot yellow sun.

Freya Nedderman (12)
St Gerard's School Trust, Bangor

My Magic Box
(Based on 'Magic Box' by Kit Wright)

I will put in my box . . .

All of my friends,
The sun and the moon
And a shooting star.

I will put in my box . . .

Water from the Atlantic when I swam in it,
A picture of my dogs
And my ruby necklace from my grandmother.

I will put in my box . . .

An eagle of Africa,
The sphinx and the pyramids when I saw them
And money to help the poor.

My box contains the love,
Everything to help everybody
And the whole world.

My box is made of rubies, gold and stars,
It has hinges made from the Atlantic Ocean.

In my box I will save the world,
I will save people
And I will bring peace to the world in
My magic box!

Apryl Fell (12)
St Gerard's School Trust, Bangor

My Magic Box
(Based on 'Magic Box' by Kit Wright)

I will put in my box . . .

The paw of a dog,
The tooth of a mammoth,
The blood of a Cyclops as a cure for all diseases.

I will put in my box . . .

The happy memories of my past,
The sad memories that appear in my future,
The quietness I suffer during school.

I will put in my box . . .

The egg of an elephant escaping from a cage,
The horrible teachers who set us homework,
The emptiness of time itself.

My box is fashioned from sand itself,
With eggs on the lid and the corners are burnt,
Then toss it away into the sea,
So everyone can share in my dreams.

I will put in my box . . .

Nothing at all,
Just peace,
All for me.

Matthew Motley (12)
St Gerard's School Trust, Bangor

The Magic Box
(Based on 'Magic Box' by Kit Wright)

I will put in the box . . .

A cheer from the crowd when we score a goal,
A boo when the other team scores a try,
When I crash the snare drum on my drum kit.

I will put in the box . . .

When the stars are bouncing upon me,
The water swishing in the sea,
A fish jumping up and down to eat the flies.

I will put in the box . . .

The first words of a baby,
The last words of an old person
And a person who can sing *great*.

I will put in my box . . .

A cat friends with a dog,
An evil witch with a white cat
And a good witch with a black cat.

My box is nice like chocolate, gold and money,
With food and secrets on the ceiling
And doors made out of torn in half homework.

I shall play football in my box,
Against the world's best players,
In the best stadiums in the world
And beat all of them.

Ben Jones (12)
St Gerard's School Trust, Bangor

My Box
(Based on 'Magic Box' by Kit Wright)

I'll put in my box . . .

The rumbling sea
And the venom of a serpent to poison the world.

I'll put in my box . . .

The thumping of a dark galloping horse
And the howling of the cold wind.

I'll put in my box . . .

The feel of the terror of the poor girl
Crying in the corner
And the screaming mother who has lost her child.

I'll put in my box . . .

The blood of a newborn baby
And delicate skin of a black rose.

I'll put in my box . . .

The pain of a young person dying in the shadows
And the sound of a teardrop on a page.

I'll live, cry and die in my box,
With rose petals on the floor,
In my dark silky box.

Anna Mathiesen (12)
St Gerard's School Trust, Bangor

Tigers

Being hunted to extinction,
Not many left now,
Many tigers there were,
Only a handful to care for.

Tigers, beautiful in their own way,
Big, agile and fast.

Watching you with their huge amber eyes,
Staring at you,
Waiting . . .

Waiting . . .
Waiting for the perfect moment,
The perfect moment to leap and strike.

This was what once had been,
Now they must be kept in zoos,
No longer can they live alone,
In the wilderness,
Free to do as they please.

Humans came and drove them to extinction,
Now we must try and save them,
Or another beautiful animal will be lost,
It is our fault that
All
The beautiful animals are lost.

Morfydd Thomas (13)
St Gerard's School Trust, Bangor

Pandas

Panda, large and kind looking,
Their fluffy fur,
Large innocent eyes.

Lost from our world.

Tree after tree,
Is falling to the ground,
Forest after forest,
Has become history.

Pandas close to being history.

Bamboo becomes scarce,
Pandas starve,
Their incredible stare . . .
May never be seen again.

Extinction becoming closer.

Zoos may have two,
The wild may have a hundred
But . . .
Is this enough
To save the panda?

We're losing them,
People need houses,
Well so do pandas,
We're cutting down their habitats,
So people can live in luxury.

Habitats lost,
Pandas lost.

Katrina Jenkinson (13)
St Gerard's School Trust, Bangor

I See A Tiger

I see a tiger,
Crouching in the dry grass,
Watching and waiting,
Suddenly she is sprinting across the desert,
No more is she disguised,
Her prey tries to get away,
The tiger is too fast,
She pounces and sinks her sharp claws,
Into the animal's body.

I see a tiger,
Her black stripes shining in the sunlight,
Lying on the dry, dusty ground,
Her cubs playing around her,
She looks so relaxed and peaceful,
She doesn't know that there are
Killers pacing the desert,
Looking for her,
To kill her.

I don't see a tiger,
The desert looks empty,
No more are there tigers roaming the desert,
No more do I see glints of silky black,
Baby cubs playing happily,
No more do I see life.

Rosie Lowe (13)
St Gerard's School Trust, Bangor

Whale Rap

Big, bold, blubber,
This animal's full of flubber,
He rules the sea,
He's a monstrosity,
But he may be gone forever.

He's big, he's blue, he's full of fat,
For him plankton is a must,
We must act fast,
As time goes past,
Before another whale bites the dust.

Rose Sutton (14)
St Gerard's School Trust, Bangor

The Panda

I am going to disappear,
There will be no happiness,
No kindness,
No joy on this Earth,
When you take that gunshot,
You are bound to lose a lot.

If you fight against the killer,
You will make the world much happier,
You will be sunk in darkness.

The panda is saved from extinction,
There will be happiness after all,
You will feel so tall,
You are bound to not fall in darkness,
Because you fought against the killer.

Tanya Duffy (13)
St Gerard's School Trust, Bangor

The Kite

The beautiful bird swoops down low,
Guarding its target.

Its yellow, beady eyes watch the unaware target,
It circles its target and waits,
Examines the area and eventually dashes down to the ground.

The target already dead and still inactive,
The kite patrols around and smells its target,
It stops and pauses, its wings confine slowly with deep care.

The kite leans forward slowly and begins to tear its prey apart
With its sharp teeth and dark, rough claws.

The kite's feast is over and all that lies on the ground
Is a pile of rotting bones.

It spreads its glorious wings out and
Takes flight into the open sky.

The sky is empty and bare in the deep part of the forest
As not many kites remain.

The famous kites are becoming extinct,
The skies are quiet, the forests are bare
But nobody seems to care.

Jessica Watters (13)
St Gerard's School Trust, Bangor

Tiger From The Past

My dear come sit down,
Shall I tell you of this beast,
A beast of such beauty,
Eyes burning bright,
You would not hear it coming,
Padding slowly up behind you,
Creeping, crawling.

My dear listen closely,
As I describe to you this beast,
Pouncing upon unsuspecting prey,
Its fur was gleaming,
The light played tricks on its coat,
Causing it to resemble dancing flames,
Burning, brilliant.

My dear do not fidget,
As I tell you of this beast,
His fangs and claws terrorised the minds
Of inferior creatures,
Their screams rang through the forest,
Screaming, squealing.

My dear I see you're eager,
For me to tell you of this beast,
It defended its young offspring,
A watchful eye on predators,
A cunning eye on prey,
Watching, waiting.

My dear I see you wondering,
Where this beast is now?
It is gone,
Its sleekness now only a memory,
It died in 2008,
Long gone.

Charlotte Taylorson-Smith-Pritchard (13)
St Gerard's School Trust, Bangor

The Panda

The panda is dying,
It spreads through the jungle,
Voices echoing, monkeys screaming,
The last in existence.

The panda is dying,
With its black and white fur,
Its dark, knowing eyes,
Gone, forever.

The panda is dying,
Its sharp teeth will chew,
The very last shoot,
Of bamboo.

The panda is dying,
What can we do?
We had our chance,
But now it has passed.

So the panda is dying,
Its eyes shut to the world,
It breathes its last breath,
Then it is no more.

The panda is dead,
Is this what we wanted?
We could have stopped it,
But we turned our backs to the world.

Jaimie Whiteley (13)
St Gerard's School Trust, Bangor

Natural Beauty

Clear blue skies, a golden sunrise,
Rivers flow freely, pure light in disguise,
Lush mountain meadows, diamond-full ghettos,
Birdsong morning, cricket-drum night,
If only, if only, it could last forever.

Then Man came along and changed this sweet song
And all of this beauty was gone,
The sky is now grey, sunrise a dismay,
The rivers are stifled by oil we lay,
What will the future hold?
We can only wait and pray.

If only, if only we could go back in time,
Change what we did,
Not in this rhyme.

Radha Patel (13)
St Gerard's School Trust, Bangor

Pride

Eyes emerald slits,
Piercing and alert,
Ears pricked forwards,
Waiting,
Breathing so softly,
Claws unsheathed,
Waiting.

Its coat striking and
Shining with brilliance,
Teeth as sharp as knives,
Waiting,
Not long to wait now,
Crouching, tail wagging,
Waiting.

Gone! With scarcely a pause,
Paws covering ground so fast,
It reaches its prey and pounces,
Teeth sinking into the flesh,
Its feeble prey struggles to free,
Itself from the claws of evil.

Its prey struggles one last time,
Then its body goes limp,
The great amber beast settles down,
To enjoy its magnificent feast,
Its heart racing with pride.

Harriet Silcocks (13)
St Gerard's School Trust, Bangor

The Hunter Or The Hunted?

Man cuts down the Earth's trees,
He cuts down on the clean air,
Man plants his rubbish in the Earth,
He plants the seed of pollution.

The hunter or the hunted?

Man destroys habitats,
He destroys his brothers and sisters - the animals,
Man builds factories,
He builds up the smoke and choking fumes.

The hunter or the hunted?

Man leaves his country but ruins others,
He leaves a trail of destruction,
Man kills the beautiful creatures,
He kills the beauty of the Earth.

The hunter or the hunted?

Man's eyes see nothing but selfish gain,
He doesn't see the pain in the tiger's amber eyes,
Man should stop his destruction,
He should open his arms and mind to heal the Earth.

The hunter or the hunted?

Laura Havens (13)
St Gerard's School Trust, Bangor

The Human Race

The planet once belonged to the animals,
But then the human race wrecked this place.

When cities grow, where do all the animals go?
I will tell you where.

We keep them as pets,
They should be running in the wild with their own child.

Some are beaten,
Some are eaten,
Some are locked in a shed.

So now you know,
What the human race,
Has done to this place,
It's a disgrace.

Alex Brown (13)
St Gerard's School Trust, Bangor

My Feelings

The glorious sunset is a spectacular red,
The blooming sky is blue,
These things are beautiful but not as beautiful as you.

Me and you have had our ups and downs,
But you're my favourite girl in my imaginary town,
I love you ever so much,
Yet the gates to my heart have slammed shut.

Sadly now you have to go but if I
Had my way, I'd say no,
Yet the power of love is as powerful as a toothpick,
I know you hate the name Nick, sadly my name's Nick.

I love you loads, yet you're going now
And I'll have to give you the goodbye bow.

Caleb Allport (12)
St Gerard's School Trust, Bangor

A Day In Llaneilian

We were in Llaneilian,
My dad and me,
Enjoying the breeze,
Looking out to sea.

Dad was cold, tired and hungry,
We watched the porpoises,
Jumping, diving, performing,
Totally wild and wonderfully free.

A picture like this,
Not often to be seen,
Oh Lord! How wonderful,
Is this really all for me?

I love my dolphins
And porpoises so wild,
I hope one day I can show,
This lovely scene to my own child.

Blanca Bennett (12)
St Gerard's School Trust, Bangor

Hallowe'en

H airy hands folding round the doorknob,
A ngry monsters coming out of their hiding places,
L urking beneath the floorboards,
L atches creaking in the dark,
O wls creeping through the sky,
W inking spiders wriggling down the walls,
E mpty people hunting for flesh,
E eak, bats squeaking in the night sky,
N ever go out in the dark, never know what you will find.

Nicole Pearson (11)
St Gerard's School Trust, Bangor

My Dog Moo

My dog Moo is black and white,
Her heart is gold, her eyes are bright.

My dog Moo is not polite,
She sometimes gives us a bit of a fright.

My dog Moo is mental sometimes,
She whirls around in the wind like chimes.

But when it gets dark and she's tired and fed,
She snuggles down in time for bed.

India Hill (12)
St Gerard's School Trust, Bangor

Whizz! Fizz! Crackle! Snap!

Whizz! Fizz! Crackle! Snap!
What on earth was that?
It is really time already?
Yes, it is dear Eddy,
Really Eddy, didn't you remember?
Now I do, it's the 5th of November.

Boom! Bang! Whirl! Fizz!
This is way better than 'Les Mis'
I've heard there's something special this year!
Yeah, they've been imported from South Korea,
Red, yellow, purple, blue,
Hey, this is so cool!

Boom! Bang! What's that?
It's only a firework Matt,
Oh! I see something coming,
It's OK, no point worrying,
Hey, look there's one red and blue,
I know, I like them too!

Hannale Niesser (11)
St Gerard's School Trust, Bangor

Sloth

A sloth hangs the wrong way up,
He spills water from his cup,
He moves slower than a snail,
Do sloth's have a tail?

A sloth hangs from a tree upside down,
He is like a funny circus clown,
He is a small furry bear like mammal,
Is he the colour of a camel?

A sloth hangs from a tree,
You know where he'll be,
Moving very, very slow,
Where can a sloth possibly go?

Phoebe Lofts (11)
St Gerard's School Trust, Bangor

Snow Fight!

As I wake up in the morning
And smell the fresh air,
I know he will be waiting,
Outside - right over there!

As he builds his snowman
And I build mine,
I throw a snowball at him,
It trickles down his side.

He shouts, 'Snow fight!'
And throws a snowball,
Full of sheep muck,
It was luck,
As I dodged out of the way.

It hit his snowman in the face
And the eye flew high
And landed in the stream.

'I know how to settle this!' he says,
'We'll have a sledge race,'
And to the hill, he led.

We skid down the hill
And both hit a rock,
We both go flying
And land with shock.

We run the rest of the hill on foot.
And we skidded,
Tripped over,
Pushed one another,
Rolled,
Jumped,
Flipped over in mid-air,
And landed,
As a draw.

Jodie Marley (11)
St Gerard's School Trust, Bangor

I Like Horses

Big horses,
Little horses,
I like them all.

Long waving tails,
Clip clop of shoes,
I just don't like cleaning,
Out all of their poos.

Dun horses,
Dark horses,
I don't mind at all.

Big waving manes,
Wide open noses,
Long twitching ears,
But they don't smell like roses.

Round horses,
Skinny horses,
I love them all.

Canter through fields,
Gallop on the beach,
The most excitement,
You could ever reach.

Olivia Roberts (11)
St Gerard's School Trust, Bangor

Fish

Fish swimming in the sea,
Sharks eat them for their tea,
Dolphins diving from the air,
Looking for their daily fare,
Whales swimming at the bottom,
Eating fish, quite a lot of them.

Different coloured fish,
Eating their own dish,
Orange, red, blue and green,
Some of the strangest fish,
You have ever seen!

Anna Jones (11)
St Gerard's School Trust, Bangor

Down In The Sea

Down in the sea,
Where the fish swim free,
You will find a rock,
If you give the rock a little push and little knock,
You'll find something brill,
Oh yes you will.

This thing you will find,
Will make your teeth grind,
For its beauty is so, so sweet,
You'll be glad when you meet,
This little treat.

Down in the sea,
Oh yes, down in the deep blue sea,
Where fish swim free.

Jessica Stanmore (11)
St Gerard's School Trust, Bangor

The Tornado

See the dark black stripe,
Coming closer and closer,
Twisting and turning,
Twirling and hurling,
Houses and trees,
Ripped and scared,
Lifted and stifled,
Dumped and destroyed.

What stirs this fury?
Whose giant hand
Whips up this chaos,
Destroying the land?

Eve Aron (12)
St Gerard's School Trust, Bangor

The Sea

The sea rocks and whiles away,
Its murky waters, its clouds of spray,
The wind whistles on its head,
The waters stirring in its bed.

Underneath a new life begins,
Two parents protecting their kins,
The creature's, lurking, moving around
Their prey, scared, unduly bound.

Above the sea, it's all unclear,
A tramp in a boat, playing a lear,
His face chalk white, his lips stone-blue,
What awaits him, he hasn't a clue.

Tom Niesser (12)
St Gerard's School Trust, Bangor

The Dark

As I walked in the dark,
I heard not a single spark,
The floorboards stirred,
Still nothing was heard,
Light shone through the door,
As I walked forth I heard a roar,
The door opened,
I froze, oh so still,
For there it stood,
So tall and fierce,
Us both in no motion,
Oh so still, oh so still . . .

Olivia Farmanbar (12)
St Gerard's School Trust, Bangor

My Niece!

Her name's Mia Brooke
And her last name's Evans,
I think she was an angel,
Sent down from the heavens.

She's five months old,
She's not got much hair,
She's wriggly to hold,
Her skin's very fair.

She's trying to laugh,
She's trying to talk,
She loves a bath,
She'd love to walk.

She sits in her pram,
Playing with her toys,
She keeps trying to eat them
And makes lots of noise.

Sarah Owen (12)
St Gerard's School Trust, Bangor

The Magic Of A Book

So many words contained in a book,
But does anyone dare to look,
Beyond what may reach the eye,
A world unexplored lies deep inside.

Magic, adventure and so much more,
All still fresh, just open the door,
Behind all those letters there is a key,
Just open the book and you will see.

Lucy Spain (12)
St Gerard's School Trust, Bangor

The Swallows

The amazing journey the swallow makes,
Through the winter and across many lakes,
The little birds fly over night and day,
They travel through many months, even May,
But when they finally stop to take a rest,
They get a chance to make their nest.

They gather their moss, straw and hay,
Having made so much effort, they're here to stay,
Their babies soon arrive,
Parents teach them how to dive,
Then the weather becomes much colder,
But now they are so much older,
The time has come that they must leave,
With a huge sigh, they do heave.

Jessica Hannah Vicars (12)
St Gerard's School Trust, Bangor

Vampires

It's time for flight,
It's time for bite,
At midnight tonight,
They are coming to fright.

They fly in the dark sky,
Someone you know could be a lie,
Don't be scared and cry,
But someone is going to die.

Whatever you do,
Don't look out the window,
Because if you do . . .
They will come for you!

Morgan Gould (12)
St Gerard's School Trust, Bangor

Fireworks

Rockets exploding in the sky,
Shooting up so very high,
Rockets booming very loud,
Blasting up to impress the crowd.

Squealers whirring are insane,
Whistling like a freight train,
Squealers whizzing through the air,
Sparkling everywhere.

Jumping Jacks hopping here and there,
Bouncing up and down.

Roman candles glittering,
Like a multicoloured light,
Roman candles gleaming like a flame,
No way are they lame.

Edward James Frost (13)
St Gerard's School Trust, Bangor

Sweets For Grandma

Sweets, sweets, the grandma treat,
Give it to her and watch her eat.

Give her a toffee and watch it get stuck,
Her teeth will stay in with a bit of luck.

Oh dear old grandma,
With your teeth you must take care,
Cos one trip to the dentist, your mouth will be bare.

Sioned Williams (12)
St Gerard's School Trust, Bangor

The Four Musketeers

They're always there for you, no matter what,
Through thick and thin,
Through smiles and tears,
They share your hopes,
They share your fears.

They're on your side no matter what,
Whoever it is,
Whatever they say,
They stop you hurting
And give support in every way.

So if you're feeling down and need a friend,
They'll be there for you,
To stop your tears,
So if you need a hug,
Don't forget to call the four musketeers.

Elin Dawson (12)
St Gerard's School Trust, Bangor

The Scary Creature

It comes out at night,
When I turn off the light,
Crawling under my bed.

Its teeth clicking,
Its nose sniffing,
It's roaring for food.

The sound it makes,
Gives me the shakes,
I'm hiding under my sheets.

It's crawling, it's moving,
Nearer and nearer,
Stop! Stop! Stop!

I tell him to go,
But I think he said no,
Its roar is louder than ever.

I've had enough,
I'm feeling quite tough,
I grab my bat and turn on the lamp.

But after all that trouble,
All I can see is my dog.

Sara Jane Jones (13)
St Gerard's School Trust, Bangor

Rooks Are Crooks!

Rooks are despicable,
Their menacing little grins,
Their horrible habits,
Too many sins!

Rooks are black,
Wicked, evil birds,
They are thieves,
Scavengers and killers,
Rooks are crooks!

Morgan Teal (12)
St Gerard's School Trust, Bangor

The Wolf

The wolf in the forest was very scary,
It was very tall and very hairy,
His teeth were as sharp as a razor blade,
Under the thick trees he laid,
He howls horribly in the night,
Giving babies a terrible fright,
The hunters try to chase him down,
He runs away with an angry frown,
Double check, the lock on the door,
For tomorrow, you might be no more.

Faizan Asad (12)
St Gerard's School Trust, Bangor

Noise

I like the noise of a crack of a bone,
I hate the noise of a shattering dome,
I like the noise of a drunk man's burp,
I hate the noise of my brother's chirp,
I like the noise of a person who's daft,
I hate the noise of a clown's laugh,
I like the noise of Hannah's non-stop talking,
I hate the noise of my brother's stalking,
I like the noise of a pouring from a cup,
I hate the noise of my brother not shutting up
And of all the sounds I hate and like,
I laugh at the sound of Homer's fright.

Aya Maria Abdulmawla (12)
St Gerard's School Trust, Bangor

I Like Noise

I like noise,
The *crack* of thunder, carried on the wind,
The *bang* of fireworks on Bonfire Night,
The *whoosh* of a train rushing by,
The *flapping* of a sail, on a warm summer day,
A *gust* of wind, scattering leaves like flies,
The *roar* of a football crowd, chanting a song,
The *horn* of a truck shocking drivers ahead,
The *belch* of Barney, in wrinkly Moe's bar,
The *call* of an eagle, echoed through the mountains,
The *blast* of a hawk at RAF Valley,
I like noise.

Jordan Anderson (11)
St Gerard's School Trust, Bangor

I Like Noise

The screeching of an eagle as it caught its prey,
The wind whooshing on a stormy day,
The crack of fireworks shooting from the docks,
The bang of thunder crashing from the sky,
The scream of a baby buzzing through my mind,
The skid of a chair along a long, dry floor
And an alarm clock ringing on a cold winter's dawn.

Wait . . . I hate noise.

Owain Fraser-Williams (12)
St Gerard's School Trust, Bangor

Shhh!

The spaces in-between your heart beating,
The calmness of the sea,
The silence of a child sleeping,
The winter snow,
The silence of a bird gliding,
The silence in a wood,
The earth moving,
The earth becoming frozen,
The silence of dead,
I like silence.

Jack Allport (12)
St Gerard's School Trust, Bangor

Whispered Wonders

Whispering wonders is waiting for a race to begin,
The silent slip in the water of a dolphin's fin,
A butterfly in the morning fluttering in the breeze
And a silent standing statue in a long everlasting freeze,
The forgotten spirit of someone in a dark alleyway
And lying in bed waiting for the next silent day.

Grace Taylorson-Smith-Pritchard (11)
St Gerard's School Trust, Bangor

Silence Is . . .

Silence is all around,
Silence is the sound of the lift coming and going,
Silence is the trees swaying in the breeze,
Silence is the tick-tock of the clocks,
Silence is the bird flying high across the sky,
Silence is the Earth moving,
Silence is the wind hitting a kite,
Silence is all around.

Jessica Waddy (11)
St Gerard's School Trust, Bangor

The Breath Of Death

A life without an open mouth,
Oh life was such a bore,
But now I am old and live down south,
My breaths feel like a chore.

My brain is gradually fading,
My ears are becoming betraying,
My mouth only gives out hardening breaths,
Meaning I am very near my death!

Bethan Mair Humphreys (11)
St Gerard's School Trust, Bangor

Noise

Noise is the loudest of all earthly things,
The *tweet* of a bird, the flap of its wings,
The *squeak* of a guinea pig, a wolf's howl,
The sound of a lion on the prowl,
The *squelch* of feet in muddy ground,
The *buzz* of a bee flying around,
The sound of wind howling through trees,
The sound of bubbles in the deep sea,
The sound of a pin hitting the floor,
The quietness after a downpour,
Noise is the quietest of all earthly things,
Because silence is the thing that does not exist.

Sacha Healey (11)
St Gerard's School Trust, Bangor

The Sounds I Love!

I love the noise!
A *crack* of lightning, a *roar* of thunder,
The wind on the prowl, blowing a blunder,
The sound of birds, tweeting a song,
Sounds of the bell, *ding-dong*!
The sound of an engine, roaring at the sky,
Birds wings flapping as they fly,
The waves crashing against the shore,
Oh, how the quiet is such a bore!

Alana Maerivoet (11)
St Gerard's School Trust, Bangor

Noise

Noise is a dog's bark,
In the early morning,
Noise is a bird's song,
In the early dawning.

Noise is a hoof,
Thudding on the ground,
Noise is a racing car,
Zooming round and round.

Noise is the crashing,
Of the waves and the sea,
Noise is the buzzing,
Of a bumblebee.

Katie Moules-Jones (11)
St Gerard's School Trust, Bangor

I Like Some Noise!

I like noise,
The laughter of children playing in the snow,
I like that noise,
The noise of a baby wailing late in the night,
I don't like that noise.

The shower of fireworks late in the night,
I like that noise,
The *creak* of the floorboards squeaking in the night,
I don't like that noise.

The *rush* of the wind flying through the trees,
I like that noise,
The *clang* of pots and pans early in the morning,
I don't like that noise,
I only like some noise!

Bryony Jayne Rodger (11)
St Gerard's School Trust, Bangor

My Box
(Based on 'Magic Box' by Kit Wright)

I will put in my box . . .

The soft canter of a dark horse,
The howl of a wolf lost in the darkness,
A golden moon enlightening the black Earth.

I will put in my box . . .

A mermaid twisting and turning through glistening water,
The giggle of a dolphin playing with a yellow fish.

I will put in my box . . .

The wings and halo of a girl angel,
The dust of a fire fairy buzzing through the bushes.

I will put in my box . . .

The thoughts of a mystical dragon,
Dry rain and wet sunshine,
Gravity in space and none on Earth.

My box is made from silver paper,
Wings and stardust.
It is drizzled with honey and butterflies hover around it.

I shall gallop through my box on the golden rolling countryside,
Then stop and admire the metallic tree with shining blossom,
Just me and the dark horse.

Becky Hill (13)
St Gerard's School Trust, Bangor

The Magic Box
(Based on 'Magic Box' by Kit Wright)

I will put in the box . . .

The big pink castle of a princess,
A bouncy castle made out of chocolate,
The magical land of fairies.

I will put in the box . . .

A pink and white marshmallow tree,
A sip out of a river of lemonade,
A bite out of a wall of shortbread biscuits.

I will put in the box . . .

A dancing ballerina in a pink dress,
The twinkling of a diamond on a ring,
A golden flower from my hair.

I will put in the box . . .

Some snow from a Christmas angel's wing,
A prince on a dolphin on the ocean,
A palm tree swishing in the exotic air of Mexico.

My box is fashioned from sand and silver
And steel corners locking the deep secrets away,
With shooting stars across the lid and the hinges
Are the feet of a belly dancer.

I shall dance in my box,
In a great theatre on a stage and roses falling at my feet,
With the audience roaring with joy.

Nia Owen (12)
St Gerard's School Trust, Bangor

My Magic Box
(Based on 'Magic Box' by Kit Wright)

In my box there will be . . .

A sting of a bumblebee,
A claw of a hawk,
A tooth of a great white shark.

In my box there will be . . .

Gold dust from a fairy,
A twinkle of a star,
(Not any star - the North Pole star)
A feather of a red kite.

In my box there will be . . .

An extra moon at night,
More stars out twinkling above the sky and . . .
The Northern Lights covering the world on
Christmas Eve.

In my box there will be . . .

The shimmer of a diamond,
The cold from the snow
And the brightness of the sun.

My box is fashioned out of the twinkle
Of the North Pole star,
Sprinkled with gold dust
And has lion cub paws as legs.

In my box . . .

I shall glide on the silver water like an elegant swan,
Then dance in winter on the frozen pond
And watch the sun set on Christmas Eve.

Claire Fell (12)
St Gerard's School Trust, Bangor

The Meaning Of Life

What is the meaning of life?
Life, life,
So easy to lose,
A mis-aimed gun,
A slip of a knife,
Maybe the meaning of life is death,
Death, the beast with a jaw of a trillion teeth.

If the meaning of life is death,
What happens when we pass away?
Do we go to God or Satan's domain
Or do we get reborn,
Or do we get scattered to the wind and rain?

The rain screams with a million trapped souls
Or maybe I'm wrong,
Maybe the meaning of life is not death
But I doubt it.

On Flander's Fields the poppies grow
From the souls of the departed,
Coloured by their noble blood
After they faded into darkness.

The light brigade charged forward,
Through Satan's mouth,
Past his evil belly
Into the kingdom of our Lord.

Dylan Davies (11)
Ysgol Gyfun Gwynllyw, Pontypool

Sorry

I never meant to hurt you,
I never meant to make you cry,
I said some mean things about you
My friend
And now my heart feels heavy and I sigh.

I know that I'm not perfect
And I know I make mistakes,
Truth and honesty is hard to find
And our friendship is not fake.

I didn't call you ugly,
I didn't say you were getting fat,
A Chinese whisper from a so-called mate,
Convinced you I said that.

I wish I had a time machine,
One that really works,
I would set the date for yesterday,
Go back and stop the hurt.

But I haven't got the easy option,
Of going back in time,
I must face up to my responsibilities,
The job of saying sorry is all mine.

I walk up to you, and you look at me
And after an awkward pause,
'I'm really sorry,' I finally say,
'I didn't think a silly joke would hurt you quite this way.'

The school bell rings to start the day,
But before we go to class,
I smile at you and you smile back,
Best friends again at last.

Grace Williams (11)
Ysgol Gyfun Gwynllyw, Pontypool

The Fire Dragon

Have you seen the fire dragon
In a rage and roar?
He wanders through the dark thick mist,
His feet bang banging on the floor.

Don't you dare go near him,
He puffs out lots of smoke,
It's written in the dragon book,
It's certain you will choke.

His big round eyes and enormous head,
If he touches you - you are dead!
You'll see the blood go drip, drip, drip,
You'll hear his teeth go click, click, click.

I wouldn't go one step on,
He's fierce I tell you - the fire dragon.

Abbie Rebecca Jones (11)
Ysgol Gyfun Gwynllyw, Pontypool

Turn Back Time

If only I could turn back time,
If only I could take it all back,
If only all those words were just a mime,
I would not have to pack.

I feel so stupid,
Let me go back to the past
And change all these things,
Back and back to the week before last.

If only there was a time machine,
That some clever scientist invented,
I can't leave now,
I can't put all these things to one side
And close the lid.

Emily Dicken (12)
Ysgol Gyfun Gwynllyw, Pontypool

Through The Eyes Of The Fishes

Round and round the fish went every day,
With her slippery, scaly skin brushing against the
Slimy plants, she glided through the tank,
They all seemed happy, in their round and round world.

The floor was covered in tiny smooth pebbles,
Pieces of coloured stones,
Fossils of long dead creatures,
Shells from a saltwater world of animals
Which the fish had never seen.

The fish looked back at the faces which peered into the tank,
They looked to see if the fish did anything new,
They saw nothing different, just the fish going round
And round and round.

She listened to the throbbing of the pump, day and night,
To the splatter of stones spat out by the other fish
And decided no more.

She wanted freedom, to find new treasures,
Make new friends,
To see the creatures who lived in shells,
She would jump,
From the round and round world to the next.

Evie Gill (11)
Ysgol Gyfun Gwynllyw, Pontypool

Through The Eyes Of A 9/11 Sufferer

I called for my secretary,
She came with a smile,
I asked her to get me,
My important file.

Suddenly it happened,
On the 94th floor,
I saw it coming,
Then there was a roar.

Everything went dark,
I heard people cough,
My desk was on top of me,
So I threw it off.

Everyone was screaming,
I tried to calm them down,
I saw the mountains of dust,
The small particles were brown.

I started to panic,
Didn't know what had happened,
People were crying
And others just stunned.

I remembered about my caring secretary,
I found her under the piles of dust,
Her eyes were closed, I checked her pulse,
Nothing was to be heard above all the fuss.

I panicked and worried,
I screamed for help,
But nobody listened,
There was no one to help.

I soon realised,
That she had gone,
Left this world
And I was alone.

I ran down the hundreds of steps,
I could hardly see where I was going,
People were shouting and screaming,
For those at the front to keep moving.

At last I got to the bottom,
The police told me to go,
It happened again to the other tower,
What was happening? I didn't know.

Headlights shone through the dust,
Like stars on a clear, dark night,
People pushed me out of the way,
I was soon out of sight.

I walked all the way home,
Noticed I was bleeding,
I rang my mum to tell her,
That I was still breathing.

Everything had happened so quickly,
Why did it have to be here?
On my filthy cheek,
I felt a single tear.

Bethan Machado (13)
Ysgol Gyfun Gwynllyw, Pontypool

The 9/11 Disaster

It was 11th September 2001, and I awoke,
I made my sandwiches and grabbed my Coke,
I kissed my wife, my children too,
I was happy and content through and through,
I walked down the road and caught a bus,
I smiled at the school kids, excited fuss,
The day was bright, the air was warm,
Little did I know the mood was to be torn.

At 8.46 on the dot,
I jumped out of my seat like a shot,
I ran up the steps and
Took a huge breath,
Not knowing that I was going to meet my death,
I jumped in the queue,
Taking out my money,
The waitress questioned kindly, 'What d'ya want honey?'

I could see something approaching from the corner of my eye,
I turned my head slowly and let out a cry.
My emotions exploded,
As the World Trade Center imploded,
My fears for my loved ones,
My wife and sons,
How the hell would they cope,
Without their father, their hope?
The end of my world,
The end of our freedom.

My life, the pain,
When will terrorists learn we're all the same?
I lie here now on the floor,
I hear nothing then only the biggest roar,
My life it seems to have come to an end,
What other tragedies will they send?

Azaria Davies-House (13)
Ysgol Gyfun Gwynllyw, Pontypool

The Wish

I sit in my corner every day listening to him shout,
All I have in my head are the things he talks about,
Under the stairs is where I weep
And where I cry myself to sleep.

I wish and wish and wish and wish that my mum were still here,
She was the only one who cared
And she was the only one whose love I shared.

People in school sit and stare and look at the things I always wear,
I'm not allowed to have new clothes,
I'm still waiting for these memories to close.

I never want to go home for I am always on my own,
Brothers and sisters I wish I had,
So I wouldn't always feel so sad.

There is only one wish that I have in my head,
A kiss from a mum as she tucks me in bed.

Saran Wyburn (13)
Ysgol Gyfun Gwynllyw, Pontypool

The Match

It's eight nil again,
So I put down my pen,
I can't bear to write anymore,
The opposition are rough,
We played really tough,
All we wanted to do was to score,
The tackles flew in,
For the first twenty min,
Then the energy levels dropped low,
The ref was kept busy
And the linesmen were dizzy,
As the teams tried to go with the flow.

The second half came,
Half the way through the game
And the manager's notebook was full,
He started to talk
And he told us to walk,
But we thought what he said was all bull,
He finished his talk
And I felt I could walk,
He gave us that much of a shoutin'
But I didn't do that,
Gave my teammates a pat
And said, 'Come on boys, we can still win!'

We ran to the field,
Adamant not to yield,
At the thought of the sound of the net,
The whistle soon went,
The ball swerved and bent,
But it went out to nought, 'I'm upset!'
I slotted it through
And the match ball it flew,
Right into Smally's stride,
We shouted to strike,
Off the end of your Nike,
Yes! Top corner . . . we still have our pride.

Yes it's eight-one,
The whistle it went,
God you should've seen the way that it bent,
Well we're happy at least,
At the end we will feast
And we had one for all that it meant!
No regrets, we all tried . . . and we run,
Stood no real chance when all's said and done,
The meaning I feel,
Has a certain appeal,
At the end of the day football's fun!

Jake Phillips (12)
Ysgol Gyfun Gwynllyw, Pontypool

Blue

Blue is the beauty which helps mankind strive,
It multiplies hope and it keeps us alive.

The volcanic texture of orbiting high,
The altitude limit, soaring the sky.

A vast subzero tundra, lapis lazuli,
An aquatic savannah, flawless and free.

Blue is the hue of eviction from life,
Of dejection, depression, banishment, strife.

The furious adrenaline which rises and falls,
Is a deep blue presence which flows through us all.

We watch out through blue-tinted windows as we,
Muse over all the sadness we see.

Blue is the midnight of our mortal years,
It intensifies tension and magnifies fears.

Our souls rapture, gentian as ice,
Our spirit's breath breezes, the beloved device.

A maritime navy, an aqua tide,
A smooth cerulean, a sky cobalt dyed.

Our lives are so dominated, so ruled by the blue,
Saddened by society, hate, lies, death, rue.

Chris Williamson (12)
Ysgol Gyfun Gwynllyw, Pontypool

Metamorphosis

As consciousness enveloped me,
The strangest of scents,
Fragrances, incinerated wood,
Excited my nose.

Now, no mattress so new,
Fingers in bone - dry dust,
Enigmatic powder in fingernails,
My eyes slowly opened.

A gaze down at my feet - talons,
So serrated, so sharp,
A reflection so shocking,
A body of feathers.

Plumage so fiery, blood-red,
Freshly shed, whose?
Blazing, radiant light blinded,
My body tingled.

Temperatures fired up from a rocket,
A flaming inferno engulfed me,
The essence of true serenity,
I was a phoenix reborn.

Jack Bell (12)
Ysgol Gyfun Gwynllyw, Pontypool

The Transformation

She has a secret,
That no one must know,
What can she do?
Where should she go?

Each and every night,
When the moon comes out,
A hideous monster she becomes,
Without a doubt.

She's had this curse,
Ever since she was seven,
How can she stop it?
Without going to Heaven?

Every dreadful night,
When she is this thing,
She has a pain in her chest,
Because her heart is breaking.

One day she decides,
She has had enough,
She goes searching for a wizard,
But it's going to be tough.

She finds the wizard,
In his mysterious cave,
He casts a spell,
To put the monster to his grave.

Carys Rose Puw (12)
Ysgol Gyfun Gwynllyw, Pontypool

The Transformation

A cold sweat runs down my back,
As I face the overwhelming view,
I'm 6 inches and alone in the world
And I don't know what to do.

Breathtaking and overshadowing sights,
I explore them with confusion,
I need somebody to help me,
Or at least find a conclusion.

Footsteps slowly enter the room,
I panic with fear,
The footsteps grow louder,
The giant is near . . .

Joanne Simms (12)
Ysgol Gyfun Gwynllyw, Pontypool

The Transformation

I am the Queen for the day,
I have to talk posh,
I have to say money,
But I want to say 'dosh'.

I am the Queen for the day,
I want to go to the chippy,
I want to look nice,
But I'm not allowed my lippy.

I am the Queen for the day,
I don't want to be anymore,
But I don't want to leave,
This palace that I adore!

Amy Davies (12)
Ysgol Gyfun Gwynllyw, Pontypool

The Meaning Of Life

Have you ever wondered why we are here?
Is it true that this is our planet?
How long will it be until we become totally extinct?
Were we supposed to have this planet to ourselves?

Was our existence a quiz set by the great master himself?
Were we supposed to survive through an ice age?
Or were we supposed to tackle a comet on its way to Earth?

Why are people and babies dying all over our world?
Was it that God needed us,
Or was it Him being selfish and taking away our loved ones?

But surely we were meant to live through the ice age,
We were to conquer the comet,
We could fight off any disease that spread among our loved
Ones and friends.

So this is my thought,
This is my worry,
Was this the meaning of life?

Megan Preece (12)
Ysgol Gyfun Gwynllyw, Pontypool

The Toy Box Doll

I was sold second-hand,
As a birthday present,
For Mr Montgomery's little girl.

She had a birthday party,
With teacakes and crisps,
Every part of it, the camera
Did not miss.

She wasn't interested in the Barbies,
Nor the books, the teddies, the game,
But when her daddy showed her me,
She was happy once again.

I remember that frightful day,
When she took me shopping,
There was a dreadful collision
And I was left hopping.

We left the shop,
I had only one leg,
When we got home,
It was replaced by a peg.

At first it was itchy,
But then it went red,
Then her mother decided
And said.

'Maybe it would be better if
We got something more wearing,
Something with a skirt and
Perhaps an earring.'

They threw me in the attic,
With all the cobwebs and dust,
All because,
I went a little bust.

I shared a box with half a train,
A threadbare jacket and some
Holiday snaps from Spain.

So there it is, my journey's ended,
In a box with some toys -
That couldn't be mended.

Gabriella Sara Jones (13)
Ysgol Gyfun Gwynllyw, Pontypool

The Meaning Of Life

Help me!
Save me from this unforgivable loneliness,
That is strangling me, gripping to my neck,
Waiting for my last breath.
Rage is bubbling inside of me,
Like a volcano ready to explode.
Someone get rid of this miserable dread,
Inside of me.
Please, tell me what life means?
I need to know!
What does it mean?
Why is it here?
How did it come?
I know, I'll guess,
Maybe it's happiness, living inside of me,
Or a spirit, keeping the world alive?
To be honest, I have no idea!
I need information,
A vision of the Earth alone,
Why is it?
Am I the only one who cares?
I cannot carry on living,
Knowing that the world is going to die!

Kathryn Kelleher (13)
Ysgol Gyfun Gwynllyw, Pontypool

Through The Eyes Of A Toddler!

I stood up with help,
My dad urged me on,
I started to walk,
My worries were all gone.

I walked to my mum,
She was so excited,
I walked back and forward,
They were delighted.

We're going on a trip,
Down to the zoo,
I look at the teddy bears,
They look back at me too.

We enter a towering building,
I sit in a big basket,
We walk past colourful walls,
My mum said I was fantastic.

When we got back,
I went up to bed,
My mum said goodnight
And gently kissed my head.

Paige Hannah Godwin (12)
Ysgol Gyfun Gwynllyw, Pontypool

Through The Eyes Of My Friend

I've always thought, I always think,
That my friend is happy,
But to my horror, I was mistaken
And I wasn't there to help her.

She was so lonely and miserable and
Had no shoulder to cry on,
She was trapped in lost thoughts of,
Hopes and dreams and was too
Frightened to tell someone.

She was hiding her true feelings,
She still is hiding her feelings,
Through a fake smile and laughter,
But at least someone knows now.

Someone that cares.

Rosie Kelleher (13)
Ysgol Gyfun Gwynllyw, Pontypool

Friendship

As the teardrops fall
I realise that it is only a drop
In the vast ocean of sorrow
The weeping will continue
It is the very flow of life.

Unwelcome are the feelings
Sorrow, grief, and betrayal
The banks overflow
The river is swollen
That river will never run dry.

The clouds have gathered
Being upset and accepting grief
Is a part of life
But how much harder does
Life need to get?
Why must we put friendship on the line?

Losing a friend
It hurts too much
It should not happen to anyone
Friendship is supposed to last
And should not weaken or expire.

Feelings could cost us so much hurt
But they are the things that make us
Human.
Friends are the same, they say
Friends make you a person.

Hollie Simon (17)
Ysgol Gyfun Llanhari, Pontyclun

Memories

The sun scalded our backs
As we trudged
Through desert sands
No one knew where we
Were going
        No one
Dared to ask.

The cold froze our bones
As we trudged
Through snow-covered undergrowth
No one stopping
To rest
        No one
Was brave enough to
Face the consequences.

The darkness burnt our eyes
As we sat
Waiting
        For death
That would soon come
No one protested
We'd all heard the screams
The screams as
No water left the taps
Protesting would prolong the
Agony
        Staring at your death
For a few hours longer
Hearing others die.

Those were our
Final memories
Screams
Green clouds from the taps
Nothing
The smiles of our deaths
As we trudged
Hand in hand
Towards the light.

Eleanor Rose West (16)
Ysgol Gyfun Llanhari, Pontyclun

Away With Words

My world is dark and airless,
Well it is if I read The Times,
My music encourages me to self-harm,
Or so The Mirror would have me believe,
My clothes are linked to depression,
Sun readers would come to understand,
I hide behind my fringe to get away from the world,
Telegraph readers have noticed,
I'm pure evil and out to destroy the world,
So News of the World decided to give a warning

But

My world is dark and airless,
So I turn on the lights and open a window,
My music encourages me to self-harm,
Yet my arms are scar free,
My clothes are linked to depression,
Why? A couple of skulls and broken hearts?
I hide behind my fringe to get away from the world,
To avoid the lies you print,
I'm pure evil and out to destroy the world,
I'm a teenager, not a terrorist, get it right!
That's right, I'm a teenager!

So why is it?

I'm the only one that realises,
How self important and chauvinistic the press really are?

Why?

Ashley John (14)
Ysgol Gyfun Llanhari, Pontyclun

Young Writers Information

We hope you have enjoyed reading this book - and that you will continue to enjoy it in the coming years.

If you like reading and writing poetry drop us a line, or give us a call, and we'll send you a free information pack.

Alternatively if you would like to order further copies of this book or any of our other titles, then please give us a call or log onto our website at www.youngwriters.co.uk

Young Writers Information
Remus House
Coltsfoot Drive
Peterborough
PE2 9JX
(01733) 890066